A YEAR OF ANGUISH
A TIME FOR MIRACLES

Karen Melander-Magoon

ISBN: 978-1-7355892-0-6

Curious Muse Press
San Francisco, California

CONTENTS

A YEAR OF ANGUISH
A TIME FOR MIRACLES

Preface

We are more than halfway through the year 2020, a year of pandemic, a year of deceit, a year of protests. We are challenged to find answers to social inequities and climate change. We are challenged to partner with nature and with all that lives on earth. We are asked to look at ways to reform our world. My poetry does not offer any answers, but writing it has given me an opportunity to explore history and science and try to understand better much of life, especially suffering and injustice.

As with many of you, I am hunkering down in isolation, studying, learning about the birds, and very grateful to be encouraged by my neighbors to play piano in the evenings. I hope above all that the world to come will be one in which we can begin to leave a new legacy of justice, equality and freedom from violence, particularly for the most oppressed and vulnerable among us.

Perhaps these poems may provide some air, water and sunshine for you beloved readers, as well as a glimpse of those things we can change to bring more light and joy to the world.

A Time for Miracles

The light is dim
The candles flicker
The oil is low
Demanding a new miracle
The Menorah is lit
The Advent Wreath is burned to wax stubble
Candles float on the Ganges
Christmas trees of pagan days
Continue to sparkle for peace
As other lights demand purchase
Commercial purchase
Thieves raid the temple
Destroyed once again
By an assassin's bullet
The wasted world is tired
Forest fires in the Amazon
Burn bushland in Australia where koalas cannot run away
Earthquakes in hurricane shattered Puerto Rico destroy
Still broken homes and cover victims in rubble
Marine life in the Mariana Trench dies of plastic cancer
Glaciers calve at alarming rates
The world cries out in pain
While rulers play games with war
Migrants drown escaping one trauma for another
Toddlers washed to shore
Lie in forever sleep
Babies separated from their mothers
Cry in desperation
While on the highway
Tents are ripped apart by the wind
Debris cast aside by nature's elements
Former occupants wander the streets
Cold and dusty
Waiting for a new pandemic
It was not meant to be
It is time for miracles

The World Has Many Faces

Americans were loved after the Second World War
Heroes to everyone who saw American films
Read our books
Thought us wise and rich
As if one adjective did not displace the other
Fear of the shoe of communism led to lacing the other shoe
Absorption in anti-communism
Those in awe of Americans in Latin America
Soon wondered what happened
As in nation by nation and country by country
Goodwill towards the United States dissipated
Guatemala, Indonesia, Cuba, Uruguay, Chile, Greece
Lost faith in the USA
Mired in its own faithlessness
Disheartened already in 1918
Failing to overturn Soviet Communism
Became obsessed with it
Leading to our own betrayals of excess
McCarthyism lies and propaganda
Creating of a former ally a new enemy
Stalin led his Communists to victory over Nazi Germany
With Churchill and Roosevelt
Yet the earth turns
Obsession creates lies and enemies
After World War II
The USA made a new war against communism
Against Soviet allies in the war
Stalin defeated Nazis
But turned on his own people
Obsessed with revolution
With enemies of the people
Who are in fact all of us, the people
The world has many faces
Yet megalomania has but one
Unrecognizable
To him who wears it

The Year 2020 Begins with Murder

The year begins with murder
And mourning of millions in Iran
For a general who was no angel
Yet until we cease to write history in blood
Represents our values of might and violence
Values we have shared
Since the beginning of our country
In a new world inhabited by people who loved the land
Burned forests to encourage growth
Grew crops and hunted animals with restraint
So the land and animals might thrive
Created an alphabet of wampum
Yet were murdered with their buffalo
So the white people could realize
Their manifest destiny of arrogance
Now we murder an Iranian general
With the same arrogance of righteousness
Justified by an impeached president
Wallowing in his own self-serving tweets
To take down a general protected by international law
To further ambitions of blood and war
The signature of a country
With 800 bases throughout the world
Ready to wreak more damage
When the people
We the people across the globe
We the people want to succor the weak
Feed the hungry
Lodge the vulnerable
Heal the sick
Create a world of peace and parity
A world of justice
A world free of war and murder
A world whose history may be written
Not in blood, but in love

Step Back from the Brink

Step back from the brink?
As if we were not already
Tumbling into chaos
From cliffs we had engineered
As crumbling edifices
Monuments to vertigo
Spinning endlessly
In winds buffeted by vaping error
Stars weep blood tears
Into ponds of darkness
Accepting our lost souls
Plunging ever further
Into Hades
A lost Charon
Navigating endlessly
To Styx and Acheron
In rivers of blood
Were Sisyphus to fold his hands
Refuse to push the rock
Endlessly upwards
Only to fall back
And repeat the effort
Eternally
Were Sisyphus to stop
His futile task
And the globus tumble
Into eternity
The greatest of tsunamis
Might roll over a universe
Beyond Olympus
Beyond Hades
Beyond the tears of angels
Beyond the brink
Of never
And all might
Begin again

Thoughts on the Moon

Veiled radiance of the moon
Softly illuminates the night sky
Fog banks roll through velvet
Layered in ragged edges
Subsumed in cloudy darkness
Hiding stars
A full moon night
Like a bowl of rice
Spills over into foggy ice
Lost behind a floating cloud of light
Riding over black skies

A Fat Hawk

A fat hawk surveys the ocean
From her perch
Upon an amorphous structure
Resembling a throne
The silent bird
Confident in her dignity
Seems to accept accolades
From ascending tiny birds

A Black Bird

A black bird surveys the neighborhood
From a telephone pole perch
The black bird with white chest is busy
Pecking ruffling cleaning
Head moving in every direction
Beak open for tiny prey
The black bird dips into a hole
Inside her pole
Now rests white belly on a hidden dent
Pumps her shoulders six times
And flies away
The telephone pole seems both
Indifferent and bereaved

Tiny Chamber Music

Two tiny birds scramble
Around their feeder
On a small bright balcony
Creating tiny chamber music
Of bird song

Meditation

I watch a child
Eyes rest
Cheeks glow
She meditates
Enviably serene
As we chase thoughts
Through metaphors of cobwebs
Expel ideas
Resist distraction
Think to conquer
Our irreverent
Unleashed mind
Pursuing its own path
The child smiles
Eyes aglow
With child
Wisdom

A New Year

A new year is upon us
Ignorant of its place
Still tidying up unspent
Or overspent moments
Shuffling a deck of months
Pondering possibilities
Dealing reluctant hands
Into anonymous piles of imponderables
Wishing expectations might prove real
Reality might prove joyous
A joy to the world kind of year
Yet here she is undressed
Unready for the stage
Make up hastily applied
Startled by the dewy newness of a new year
Waiting in the wings
Her own wings just broken out of tinsel shells
To test new flight patterns
With damp feathers
A new year dawning
Wakens primal thoughts
Of butterflies and rivers
Traces of not yet thought ideas
Wishes of grace racing to the finish
As yet unknown and uncreated
A new year waits and watches
Powerful with longing
Flexing singing muscles
On arms stretched to a new sky
Full of blue
Laced with soft clouds
Brimming with sunshine
She makes her entrance
On the stage of an anxious world
Shyly imperfect
Hesitant
Yet holy

My Grandson and his i-phone

My grandson sits with his i-phone
Immersed in scenes of Alcatraz
We visited today
Thinking of all the prisoners
Just people
Maybe who did bad things
But still people
Deserving of human care
Suffering in solitary
One man ripping a button off his shirt
To throw in the air
And then seek for it in the darkness
Of his windowless cell
In solitary confinement
Simply to remind himself he was alive
His knees bearing blisters and scars
From the constant search for his button
We saw cell over cell over cell
Reminding anyone of the redundancy
Of those occupying each room
Thinking constantly of escape
One managing to climb pipes to the roof and freedom
In 1963 the prison was closed
In 1969 the indigenous peoples took over their land, Alcatraz
Up to 400 native people lived there at one time in the 19 months
Of occupation by indigenous peoples
Who tried to buy back the island from the government
Oakes was the charismatic leader whose daughter Yvonne died
Falling three stories in the stairwell onto the concrete stairs
The movement disintegrated
Yet a light was lit among the indigenous peoples
That will never be extinguished
Even while my grandson continues
To read the history of Alcatraz on his i-phone
Saying
It is so sad

Walk into Grace

Each morning
Step into sunshine
Light in your heart
Grace in your spirit
Take one step into love
Smile at wrong
That it might be made right
Forgive always
A baby cries in the night
And cannot be comforted
Let daylight dispel her terror
Observe the birds
They feed in groups
That all may be fed
They sing
That they may find their
Companions for the day
They have forgotten rancor
For they are their song

Baby Hummingbirds

Two hummingbirds hatch
Tiny fuzz in a transparent gauze shell
Like an empty walnut shell
Made of cobwebs warmed by their mother
Fed tiny things till they emerge
As feathered fledglings on wings
Propelled in dizzy circles
Flying quickly
Away

Constructs to be Dismantled

Evil is a construct
To be dismantled
To be torn down
Into the pit of earth
And rebuilt with the timber of love
Hate is a construct
To be removed with new ideas
Of reconciliation
Jealousy is a construct
To be undone
With a realization
Of our common yearning for belonging
A common euphoria
For all that is good and beautiful
Gratitude for the gift of labor
The gift of thought
Of science and art
Rain and sunshine
The gift of each day
The gift of love

A Step into Faith

Martin Luther King, Jr.
Would have us take a first step
Onto a staircase of faith
Faith in humanity
Faith in love
Faith in possibilities
Far beyond our simple vision
He would have us believe
In the reality of justice
The reality of love
The reality of possibilities
We can realize
Walking up the staircase of faith
Together

A River of Truth

His was a river of truth
Inviting us to swim in truth
Inviting us to wade through
Waters of truth
To stand in the waterfall of truth
And let truth wash down on us
And drench us with veracity
Drench us with the waters of integrity
Until we are truly baptized in righteousness
Truth waits for us on the shore
Washes up each day
Bathes our feet
As Mary bathed the feet of Jesus
Its waters flow through us
Around and in us
Its depth is endless
We need only accept
The waters of truth
And remain washed
In rivers
Of wisdom
And love
Until the whole world
Is washed
And renewed
In truth

Looking for His Echo

I wonder if the caterpillar knows
If the flower knows
If the hummingbird knows
If the trees outside my window know
I wonder if springtime knows
When it is time to regenerate
Time to obey life's urges
To nestle, to bud, to blossom, to love
I wonder if the moon knows
To pull the tides
The fruit knows to drop
Before winter snows freeze its essence
If the bird knows to sing his heart out
In the avocado tree at dawn
If he knows to sing and sing and sing
And after his song
To fly across the garden
Looking for his echo

Embrace

Yin and yang
Lover and beloved
Dual consciousness
Awareness and mindfulness
Relationship the great equalizer
Loyalty to an idea of mutuality
The paw of the cat embracing its tail
A circle of contentment
The bird song echoed in its mate
Clouds mingling to face the sun
Microbes clinging to mist
Making rain
That all the world may thrive
Green grows green
Pushing buds and flowers
To open to bees and hummingbirds
Whirring gently
Dolphins spin
Unmindful of their spinning
As whales spout
Unmindful of their spouting
Baby mammals rest upon their backs
Tides enter and exit
Intuitively
In response to the moon
The earth smiles on one lunar plain
While the other basks in the universe
Dark and mysterious
Yin and yang
Light and shadow
Embrace of opposites
Finding harmony

Grief

Grief resides in clouds
Heavy with incipient rain
Held in heaven's embrace
Grief resides in rivers
Flowing to oceans of sorrow
Held in earth's bowl of tears
Grief comes silently
On paws of cats
Soft and remembering
Grief waits
For signs of a presence
For a touch from the past
A caress of the wind
Grief sits quietly
In all places
Where love
Once smiled
Grief sings
In the song of the oboe
Warmth of wood and reed
Spinning hollow thoughts
Into sweet honey
Dripping sorrow
Into a heart
Full of remembrance

Where is time?

Where is time
Where did it hide?
Where did it go?
Did it take my heart
Or a part of me?
Where is time?
Where is lost time?
Can I find it in the air?
Find it in water?
In earth?
Where is time?
Did it ride away
On a chariot of wisdom?
Or on a boat
Paddling into eternity?
Did it lose its way
Looking for my heart
To hold it
Forever?

Inquiline

Inquiline living
A moth child
Snuggling in
A special gall
Curled into her
Willow leaf
Woodpecker
Snuggling in his tree
Knocking on the door
Of squirrel inquilines
Host and guest
In inquiline amity

Air Earth Water

Air earth water
Words to think on
Lightness depth life
Body of the mother
Stretching curled
Buffeted by winds
Veins exploited
Blood and rock
Fracked
Yet planetary orbits
Rock throughout
The galaxy
Moon rises
Pulls tides
Stars illuminate
Night skies
Blanketing mother earth
Bejeweled with diamonds

Blocks of Houses

Blocks of houses
March across the street
Topped by dancing chimneys
The smallest one
Leaning against the middle chimney
Tops and bottoms
Smudged with soot
Cable wires decorating blocks
Like a necklace
Draped artistically
Across a noble house
Surveying the street
With dark windows
Eyelashes of eaves
Punctuated with dark lanterns
Reaching out from
Wrought iron arms
Blocks of houses
Now hang suspended in fog
Drifting slow motion
Across pale windows
Fingers of spun sugar
Held like child's hands
Over building block faces
Robotically square
Yet suggesting fragile questions
Punctuated by wings
Of a dark bird
Flying past
Dancing chimneys

The Beginning of Land Property

Joseph Gidden
Born January 18, 1813
Made barbed wire
From an old coffee mill
Chopped up pieces
Attached to wire
Marked the beginning of
Property demarcations
In the west
The beginning of fast boundaries
Of plots of land
Marked the end of the civilization
Of native peoples
Marked the end of the wide prairie
The end of land
Belonging to everyone
The end of communal
Civilization
Built on sharing
Of the land
Perhaps the end
Of civilization
As it was meant to be
The end of a sentence
Punctuated by the pieces
Of an old coffee mill
Pieces of
Barbed wire
Scratching
Painfully
A final signature
Without date
Without place
The beginning
Of empty treaties
And empty greed

The Skeptic

The skeptic
Poisonous when septic
In declining positive
Possibilities of
Whatever nature
Naturally skeptical
Without allowing
Non-septic cynicism
To prevail as possible
Truth seeking sin qua non
Of voracious veracity
Avoiding septic sinking
Into pitiful pits of poison
Pontificating on putrefaction
As singular truth
Sin ti
Without you
Without
Redemption
To ally
Skeptic
Despair

An Olive Tree

An olive tree
Volunteered within a pot
On my tiny balcony
First sprouting avid green
Then waving graciously
Unaware of its heritage
Thinking itself a weed
Until it grew tall
Within its pot
Allowing gravity
To hold its sway
To bend it towards
The balustrade
Becoming one with
Metal struts
Begging to be made straight
Yet unable to surrender
Its bent nature
Succumbing finally
To its origin
A blessed olive
Drying sadly
In its pot
Upon my balcony

Master Class

The master cellist
Listens to students
Playing often masterly
Upon their instruments
Offering ideas of string
And fingers
Muscles back and arm
Fingers wrists
Light firm flexible
Explosive renderings
Long bow pianissimo
Vibrato in fingers and wrist
Changing as the music changes
Cello trills imitating the voice
Bottom note or top first
Depending on sequence
On scale
Always determined by music
I did not play this
As a young cellist
He says
Because it was too hard
I hear him feeding the student
The idea the challenge
She will do it
She can do it beautifully
The art of the teacher
Humility and
Affirmation
The next generation
Of masters
The next generation
Of music

Hummingbird

Hummingbird
Balances on wings
Making figure eights
Tiny tail like a rudder
Decorates her ¼ cup nest
Nourishes her children
Hatching one inch long
After three weeks
Crawling from their eggshells
Twenty days and more
Mommy hummingbird
Feeds her babies
When they pop out
Of their nest
She leaves them
To grow down
And feathers
But still
Comes back to protect her fledglings
Covering them in a storm
Drinking nectar
And tiny insects
We cannot see
Traveling thousands of miles
Migrating
Brushing off rain
Like a dog
And wind
Like a bolt
Of tiny beauty
Honing in to breed
And hatch and protect
New fledglings
In mini nests

Ancestors and Saints

My husband is a saint
He is gone and yet
He is here
Emanating goodness
Peace kindness love
I miss him less
Knowing he is here
I used to absorb him
In my thoughts
And dreams
Now we see face to face
Or soul to soul
The wind holds him
He rises from the ocean
With the mist and fog
Flows in the sunset
Sparkles in the dew
Or the breath of clouds
Sings with the dawn
Bows with the saplings
Glides into my heart
And rests in me
As do all our loved ones
One with ancestors
With a lineage of love
Stretching far beyond
And deep within
All space

Mozart Birthday

They played Mozart
For his birthday in January
He would have laughed with them
As they took joy in each other
Joining or completing a new phrase
Clarinet into violin into cello
Threading music into music
Measure into measure
Life into magic

Lost and found

The staircase traveled into nowhere
Wondering where it used to go
Before the roof exploded
When it lost its way
In fire and questions
Now welcoming
Tiny birds
Pecking cheerfully
Along its steps and
Diligently
Among the cinders
Finding nesting places
Hidden in burnt eaves

Camelian Coronavirus

The dromedary camel
Gave us our common cold
Originally a coronavirus
Wild animals in Wuhan
Gave us a new coronavirus
Like those named MERS and SARS
Coronaviruses
Lethal sometimes
When new
But maybe
Destined to become
Another
Common
Cold
To be endured
With mundane agents
Tissues
And Vitamin C
But now
To be fought
With masks
And distancing

Lion

Heracles slew the lion
The first of his labors
Demanded of jealous Hera
Who after she had driven him mad
Driven him to kill his wife and children
Became Apollo's voice
At the oracle of Delphi
To advise Heracles
At her living stream
To work for
Mycenae's king
He was charged to kill the lion
Whose women
Held hostage by the maned beast
Became themselves lions
Devouring those who wished
To slay their host
Heracles placed a stone at one end
Of the lion's den
Entering the second gap
To charge the lion
And strangle him
With his cloak of lion fur
He cut with the claw of the lion
And yet
History remembers the beautiful beast
Not as predator but
As king
Heroic in stature and mane
His lioness the protector
Mother to the jungle
Guardian of the forest
Worthy of his realm
Greater than the myth
Of Heracles

Wounded Knee 1890

Shuffling ghost dance
Calling for the bison and the spirits of ancestors
To return
Return to family
Return to peace
Return to the Lakota circle
Cherish the land
Shuffling ghost dance
Soon to be the dance of new ghosts
Massacred by US military
Fearful of the dance of the Lakotas
The dance for peace and the return
Of their ancestors and their bison
A deaf man protects his rifle the military would steal
When it goes off, the massacre begins
Women and children are not spared
A baby nurses on his dead mother's body
The US military spare no one
Perhaps 300 of the 350 gathered are killed
The number matters little
The bodies could not be retrieved easily
As the winter cold froze them
A massacre frozen in place
Shuffling ghosts care little
About apologies from Congress
As their lands continue to be raped
By pipelines and white dominion
Their waters contaminated by US incursions
Oblivious of treaties
Oblivious of massacres
The blood of the native
Continues to flow through cracks in the land
Owned by no one
But the Great Spirit

America's Broken Heart

Is the broken heart of America operable?
Do we open her heart to sew it together again
With the thread of equity?
Will compassion find its way into a needle
Piercing her very soul
Is she sorry for the theft
Of her land and people
Is she victim as well as perpetrator of sorrow?
Who is America?
What are her deepest regrets?
How can she apologize to her ancestors
Whom she never acknowledged
But systematically cleansed from the land
As the land itself came under her dominion
And she learned to steal persons and property
Finance her capitalism with slaves from Africa
Who is America?
Who are her children?
Those who seek nourishment from her soil and streams
While destroying them as a child does
Seeking forgiveness
Excused again by the mother
As if they know not what they do
Punished by fire, flood and disease
While the land brings forth frogs
Yea even into the king's chambers
America seeks a new heart
The old one far too broken
And yet her planet
Now has a small new moon
Just a visitor
But one who might auger
A new beginning
A healing
If only America's children
Might look up and seek redemption

A Leaf

A single leaf hangs
Among the pulsing tiny bulbs of springtime
A single leaf
Crisp and brown
Hangs
A poem to winter
A poem to a past springtime
A single leaf hangs on
Unaware of its battle
With the wind
Lifting it
Bathing its face
To spin
Spinning
Spinning
Past the buds
Into a never sky

Botanical Garden

Magnolia sings
Squirrel scuttles
Azalea bows gently
Wind blows drumming twigs
Myriad birds tweet lustily
Ducks bend over ponds
As wide spanned wings
Soar across darkened water
Muddied by diving mallards
Tall redwoods
Ladders to the skies
Demand our eyes
Look up to the tiniest branches
Imagining ourselves as squirrels
Able to climb and jump
Among the *sempervirens*
Reaching to the sun

Corona 1

Homeless lie in bundles
On wealthy streets
On steps of shuttered shops
Folded into ragged blankets
Hearing they
Must sing happy birthday
Twice when they
Wash their hands
Laughing at the incongruity
Of hygiene
On the streets of San Francisco
Hearing that a cough or a fever
Could mean death
Yet strangely unconcerned
Knowing
Life is like that

Corona 2

One thinks of
Communicating
When touch is feared
Isolation
Self- quarantine
Heart left on emptied
Grocery shelves
Where cleanser
And toilet paper
Have been removed
For hoarding
Lonely heart
Left waiting
Unneeded
Unnecessary
Drying out
On empty shelves

Sanctions Kill

Millions die due to US sanctions
Our sanctions kill
From Iraq to Venezuela
40,000 dead
Unable to access medicine and care
For two years
Sanctions kill in Zimbabwe
Unable to respond with medicines and vaccines
Respond to cholera
To Cyclone Idai
Now Covid 19 threatens entire populations
Deprived of heath care
Respiratory aids, test kits, medicine
Sanctions kill
Cuba's massive efforts
To aid the vulnerable
Throughout the world
Do not suffice
To allay damage
From US sanctions
Sanctions kill
The most inhumane
Weapon of war
Sanctions against
Vulnerable populations
Our hands
The hands of Uncle Sam
Are bloodied
And will not be cleansed
Out, out damned spot
How much more damning
Than the blood of Duncan
Are the countless victims
Of US sanctions

Virus

Shadows follow shadows
Through empty streets
Ghosts of glassware
Converse in empty restaurants
Stems remain distanced
Mouths untouched
No echo of clinking crystal
Glassware quarantined
Against the night
Coldly displayed
On pristine cloths
Under candelabras
Illuminating ephemeral moments
Wandering shadows
Conscious of space and distance
Question essence
Wait for soft paws
Of a purring miasma
Asymptomatic of nothing
Heightened temperatures
Peer through
Rooms of city streets
Coughing mildly
Blanketed bundles
Curl in corners
Under shadows
Long shadows
Stretching far beyond
Defining tomorrow
In inexplicable
Tenderness
Of loss

Covid 19 Requiem

Sylphs stretch themselves in corners
Sliding under incipient rosebuds
Careful of thorns
Cocoons await a finger of sun
To transform them into naiads
Golden hands of dryads
Grow green upon their naked limbs
Nymphs blow sweetly through spruce
Crevices of fuzzy spirit wakening
To forest shadows
Lurking vestiges of illness
Sing startle in the warm breeze
Hiding from the sun's embrace
Yet caught in her warmth
Succumb to beckoning earth
Burying remnants of Corona dust
Rusty coffins made of winter's debris
Huddled hubris of yesterday's ill wind
Crushed beneath a naiad's step
Dancing now in perfumed grace
Racing to embrace the spring

Equinox March 2020

Waiting for the equinox
Waiting for balance
Time of Noruz
Time of awakening
Balancing
As spring resets the scales
We ask for redemption
In times of plague
The world turns
Sunshine warms and waits
For shadows to dissipate
And hope to gather
Fears of contagion
Govern our actions
We distance ourselves
From others
Yet know
Only in community
Can we survive
So we light candles
Within our hearts
Warm the world
In prayer
And await
The equinox
Of hope

Rehearsal for Springtime

The birds sang out their hearts this morning
The bees tried to pollinate dead leaves
Practicing for springtime blossoms
Hummingbirds spun vertically mid air
Then disappeared with unimaginable speed
Sun beat down in bright happiness
Oblivious of contagion
Keeping her distance
While the rest of the world sheltered in place
Tracing the graph of sunshine
As that of plague
Like the stock market
Volatile and uncertain

Views of the Street on March 19, 2020

Out on the street
The 7 am jogger is absent
As was the 5 am skateboarder
The streets are strangely silent
The shuffling man on his cane appears
Unperturbed by the changing scene
I can set my clock with his walk
Tick tock
Years ago a cock
Might have crowed
Around this time
Time is the one
Constant
In a strange new world

The Ocean Forgives

The Ocean forgives
Inexhaustible ocean
Teeming energy
Witness to eons
Endless tides
Obeying the moon
Speechless and alone
Washing over a world
Deep with mystery
Yet shallow enough
For tidepools and tiny creatures
Landmasses great enough
For human civilizations
To thrive and stumble
Plunder wealth
Survive disease
Seek solace
Perhaps enlightenment
Beside an ocean
Indifferent and sovereign
Embracing whales
And small fish
Gentle with children
And their fragile
Sandcastles
Challenged with poisons
And human garbage
Insulting her mighty waves
Yet she the mother
Awash with beauty
Knows only
To accept
And to forgive
To love
And obey the moon

Covid 19

Streets are empty
I walk to the bay
Where seagulls hold court
Taking up spaces
At the railings
Empty of tourists
Streetcars rattle by
Empty of passengers
The bay is still
But for one duck
Diving
And a sea lion
Surveying the shore
Listening perhaps
For his friends
Barking on their platform
Near an empty
Pier 39

Making Do

Birds fly
Pigeons strut
Wild parrots squawk
Green careening
Over blue
Cold yet cloudless
Still and waiting
One rests briefly
Scratching absently
At concrete
Expecting sand
And yet unmoved
By absent grains
Making do
With all that is
As we must
All
Make do

Socially distance

Speak politely with the furniture
Pile the pillows just so
Talk to the refrigerator if you must
Tell it/her/him/them thank you
For taking care of the goodies
Maybe too many sometimes
But these are special times
Be kind to the furniture
You never know
When it will return the favor

Manna

The world grieves
Yet acts to contain its grief
By preserving life
Containing loss
So that we may endure
Hope is a thing with wings
Promise a destiny
That holds hope for more promises
More moments of endurance
More wings to carry us
Into the lands that hope offers
Built on little victories
That sustain
That give us toeholds
Into the next hope
Trees send tendrils under forest tundra
Bringing sustenance and promise
Extending unto the next forest
Unto the next generation
The language of hope
Speaks to us in grief and joy
The deep tendrils of growth
Carry sorrow and renewal
Loss and victory
Forcing us to knead our grief
Until it becomes the manna
Of regeneration

A Time of Plague

Hamin Mangha
Miauzigou
Forgotten names
Scenes of devastating plague
7,000 years ago
In two cities of northeastern China
No generation spared
Children adults elders
Men women
Suffered
Died
Buried in mass graves
In Hamin Mangha
Bodies stuffed in an edifice
Later burned
Another mass burial in Miaozigou
Prehistoric cities deserted
Forgotten
Memories buried in clay and ash
Later in Greece
In times of war
Peloponnesian War
One hundred thousand people
Died in Athens
Forced by Sparta
To live tightly together
Behind long walls
Died of a new epidemic
Burning red eyes and tongues
And inner organs
Yet the war continued
Until Athens capitulated 404 BCE
Two years before Sophocles died
Sparta was lenient with Athens
The Greek era of philosophers
Enjoyed the end of war and plague
Gave us teachers
Socrates Plato Aristotle
Yet wars brought to Rome

Antonine Plague
Early smallpox killed five million
One hundred fifty years
Before our greatest teacher
Walked the face of earth
Recalibrating our calendars
Just two more centuries before
The Plague of Cyprian devastated Rome
Killing 5,000 each day
Covering mass graves in lime to disinfect
A mass disease of the bowels
Called by St. Cyprian the end of the world
And yet we were still to face Bubonic Plague
Called Justinian after the Byzantine emperor
Who built the Hagia Sophia in Constantinople
His empire faded
While Hagia Sophia lived on
Christian then Muslim
The Black Death walked
From Asia to Europe
Leaving mass graves in its wake
Wiping out half of Europe
Riding on the backs of infected rodents
Yet ushering in a better life
For those who survived
Whose work was needed and
Destroyed serfdom in Europe
While farther south in Mexico
Another plague arrived
Cocolitzli hemorrhagic viral fever
Now morphing into Typhoid
And vestiges of Salmonella
And multiple diseases
Brought by European conquerors
Nearly wiping out Aztec and Mayan peoples
Gave the new world to Cortes and Pizarro
Later Britain, Portugal and the Netherlands
The Black Death of 1665
Drove Charles II out of London
While the Pied Piper of Hamlin

Led the children to the mountain
And infested rats out of the city
Yet Marseille had its Plague
And Russia under Catherine the Great
The new world of America
Found its own pestilence
In the mosquito
Bringing yellow fever to Philadelphia
Our capital in 1793
Later malaria and influenza
Polio, then AIDS
Cancer and unusual viruses
Avian flus, H1N1, Swine flu, Ebola
MERS, SARS
Now Covid 19
The eternal search for vaccines
For each new scourge
That we may learn and cure
Learn and prevent
Isolate, practice social distancing
To avoid contagious viruses
To be neither receiver nor transmitter
Fighting a scourge
Whose vector is unknown
Immunities not understood
Ubiquitous possible contagion
Waiting always waiting backstage
For a cue to enter
We wait too
Helping where we can
But mostly we wait

Kawasaki Disease May 17, 2020

Novel coronavirus
Said to leave children alone
Now wears a new mantel
Kawasaki
Like Athens Plague
Affecting Spartans in close quarters
Mysterious
Unlike any other plague
Red tongues
Enflamed intestines
Coming as a scourge
Then abating
For lack of hosts
Kawasaki
Riding on the skirts of Covid
Reaches out for children
Like a viper
As we scream stop
Our children are sacred
Let us save our children
Let us bury our pandemics
So they will not rise again
Covid. Kawakasaki
Let there be no more new names
No more plagues
Let miasma turn to sweet clean breath
Let earth restore itself
Restore its own
That we and our own children
May be healed
And learn to heal

Garden Scene

A mockingbird practices his repertoire
At the top of the highest tree in the garden
Trilling to his hummingbird friends
Spinning ecstatically in the nearby pine
Swooping to the tiny apple tree
Just beginning to blossom
Lemons hang everywhere
Filling the garden with their pungent scent
Sheltering tiny new roses
Children wander the narrow paths
Small plastic pails ready to gather marvels
Sparrows hang on low lying branches
Cocking their heads in the wind
Catching miniscule bugs
Tugging at their own feathers
Beaks diligently pecking and cleaning
While the mockingbird reigns
With brilliant eclectic melodies

Silent City

A cloud hides behind the city scape
Uncertain of her destiny
As afternoon creeps slowly over houses
Sheltering families waiting in isolation
Birds call into silent streets
Flitting over wires poles chimneys
Cats gaze from dark windows
A single siren breaks the stillness
Heralding fire engine or ambulance
A reminder of possible emergency
Or just a rogue horn
Wanting to be heard
In a silent city

Jeanne Baret

Born 1740 impoverished in Burgundy
An orphan who made her way
Learning literature and botany
Dressed as a man
Circumnavigating the world
On the vessel Bougainville
While she nursed Commerson
Whom she loved
Discovering myriad plants
Among them one named for the ship Bougainville
When Commerson died in Mauritius
Jeanne worked as barkeeper
Married and returned to France
Recognized for helping discover
Countless plants on her global voyage
And as the first woman to circumnavigate our planet
Remember Jeanne Baret
When you admire the beautiful Bougainville
A flower she discovered
On her epic global voyage
And named for her ship

Stella Fights Filthy Water

Stella was eleven
In Nova Scotia
Her mom said
She couldn't swim
In the river beside their house
Her mom said homes fed the river
With straight pipes
Pipes with no filter
Shooting sewage into the river
Horrified
Stella put a sign on the river
Contaminated with Fecal Material
Do not swim
Later placed her warnings on Facebook
Community and government woke up
Banned straight pipes
Today a 15 million dollar project
Eliminating straight pipes
Cleans up the Le Havre River
Stella has brought her message
All over Canada
People pay attention
Kids can make a difference

The City Waits

It is raining this morning
As people remain in their houses
The little old man with his cane
Still walks outside
On his morning exercise
As he always has
Birds still coo scream or sing
Over the damp city streets
A few cars putter down Columbus Street
A rare bus rattles by
Mostly silence
As the city waits
For the invisible virus
The most unwanted immigrant
No race no face no gender
To disappear

Tiny Haven Views Empty City

Pigeons mumble on the balcony
Quietly cooing
Enjoying the scent of basil
A lone gull
Refugee from the bay
Floats over empty streets

Sky Moments

Stars are invisible
Clouds cover diamond displays
Moon hides
Uncomfortable with social distancing
Birds flutter together
Sharing insects
Raindrops congregate in clusters
On my window
A veil settles on the city
Singing sonnets
To a sleeping moon
Night hides behind silk
Settling into folds of velvet
Scattering lullabies
A tiny apple tree
Shyly garlanded
With new blossoms
Welcomes the night's
Gentle poetry
As her hummingbird tenants
Seek their nest
Blanketed in
Their own soft down

Wampanoag Betrayal

Wampanoag land
Sacred
Held in trust for mother earth
Holding tribes who first aided
Pilgrims coming to the new land
Gave the new guests to the land
The feast of Thanksgiving
Yet were betrayed
And again betrayed
By the guests they welcomed
Who created a government of greed
That only wanted land and goods
For themselves
Denigrated the natives
Stole their land
Claimed their casinos
Built by the Wampanoag
To pay for education
And health care
For their children
And children's children
So they might live
On their sacred land
Fish its streams
Protect its forests
Forever
Until forever became lost
In betrayal
Of a sacred trust
With mother earth

The Shadow Walks

The shadow walks
Looking over its shoulder
At wisps of never
Carrying flowers of the night
Held tightly to its chest
Releasing perfumes
Of silent song

Pillows

In French they call ears pillows
As we speak of pillows
As voices
Pillow talk
Secrets tossed in the air
In pillow fights
Soft secrets of night
Or early morning
Forgotten memories
Hidden in the creases
Of feather pillows
Crushed ideas
Tumbled aloft
Or on window sills
To air out
Soft sorrows
Dampening linen
Soft thoughts
Dreaming joy
In pillow
Remembrance
Pillow ears
Pillow talk
Pillows

Spring in Times of Covid

Sun blazes on city streets
A new ozone hole gapes over the Arctic
Jupiter Saturn Mars over Venus and Mercury precede the sunrise
This pre-Easter week awaits palms and death and hallelujahs
When city streets are nearly empty
People wait in line to enter grocery stores
Obeying mandates for social distancing to prevent contagion
Families worry about paying bills
Stores are closed and businesses closed
Live entertainment forbidden
A different springtime peeks around the corner
A silent spring for human activity
While birds in blooming public gardens
Call exuberantly for mates
Puffed chests exuding angelic trills
Nature breathes contentedly
Factories and fracking approach a standstill
The air almost clean
Fish swim again in Venice canals
Once grey cities fill their lungs with fresh air
Yet people die from lung challenging viruses
High fever and breathlessness
Death and Easter
Infection and resurrection
Hands of nature held in prayer
Reach over her own planet
Hoping for renaissance and renewal
Rebirth of society into a new social order of healing
Rid not only of virus but of greed
Not only of disease but of hatred of the other
A new social order rid of lies
Rid of racism xenophobia capitalism privatization of nature
Rid of hierarchy and hate
A society worthy of the blazing, giving and forgiving sun of life

Twilight of Capitalism

A grey carpet of empty streets rolls out
From valleys to mountains
A social structure hollowed out by corporations
Resounds in dull thuds under the plodding feet
Of masked walkers
Phantoms of the people
Escaping sheltered spaces
Carry bags of toilet paper
From here to there
Remnants of recycled trees
Scream freedom
Years of imperial looting
Leave a western people void
Unprepared by apathetic leaders
To protect against a crisis
Pandemic smiles at ready hosts
Riding on their shoulders
Sliding into lungs to cough
Raising temperatures to fever highs
Clogging pipes to suffocate
Until it is too late, too late
Pandemic smiles already gone
To swing upon another gate
Another host another dawn
To warm the heart of any virus
Looking for a home to mate
A place to rest and duplicate
A needy hollow country begs
Continuing on hollow legs
To ask for what it will not give
Without a map on how to live
And succor those in greater need
Instead demands as if deserving
From those it should itself be serving

Pink Moon of April

A pink moon hides behind rainclouds
Moist evening veils shrouding her radiance
Rose petals float like butterfly wings
Tinged with gold for a moment
Then submerged in shadow
Moon of April sings a song of sleep
Wakening the hibernating earth
The calling birds and teeming fish
Choir of distant mermaids
Slumbering still in ocean depths
Reach for their lunar goddess
Hiding as she slides across night sky

Tinderbox

The country is mourning its dead
The people shelter in place
Cease going to work
Hide from the virus
So that they may not fall ill
And waste precious hospital resources
The country is buying guns
Thousands of guns
And the president warns of casualties
If people cannot go back to work
He speaks of war
Are we to shoot against a virus?
Or protect others
By avoiding illness?
The National Guard is waiting
Thousands strong
Waiting for someone
To strike a match
Over corpses
Drenched in oil

A Naval Hero

The captain of his ship
Named after a hero
USS Theodore Roosevelt
Raised the alarm
As his men began dying
Of Coronavirus
As his men
Five thousand strong
On a navy vessel
Became ill
Waiting to find
Sanctuary and safety
On shore
The captain of this ship
Was fired by the admiralty
For raising the alarm
For his men
Who cheered his valor
As he left the ship
So they might disembark
Never to forget
Their hero
Captain Brett Crozier
Demoted, debased
Despised and rejected
As was Christ
These days before Easter
Yet the last shall be first
In the hearts of his men
And the new virus simmers
Which will demand justice

Pandemic of Violence

Today we fight a virus
Nature's pandemic
And yet the virus of violence
Continues
In our own country
Police killings numbered 992 in 2018
In 2019 1004
In the first three months of 2020 already 238
Today, April 7, 11 killed by police before noon
Today we fight a disease
Taking thousands of lives
And yet we still manufacture weapons
That kill countless across the world
That create rubble of middle eastern countries
Who then are even more vulnerable
To virus and disease
To the effects of climate change
Engendered by our own government
In its desecration of the earth
Its greed for fossil fuels
To power its engines of
Growth
Violence and
Death

Spring Survives

Finches trill in the cool morning
Gulls fly over the city streets
Curious about dry lands, buildings and hills
Dogs patrol the streets on leashes
A strange silence reigns
Butterflies appear surprised at their own wings
Hibernating nature
Pokes her nose into the sunshine
Spring survives
Even a pandemic

Thalassic Howl

My body rises as the ocean towards you
Crumpling to meet fish and coral
Surging with waves racing towards the shore
Stretching back to seek the depths
Knowing you are there in vastness
You are the ocean
Even as mountains rise beneath me
Orogenic marine cascades
Push upwards crushing against
Plates of wild wisdom
Thalassa seeks her Pontus
Eons before oceans rose to meet Gaia
Before fire melted my bed
Angels dreamed deep power
Pounding hammers
Stampedes of surf raced earthward
Doubling back into the mighty womb
Creating re-creating primal life
Fighting chaos into servitude
Mastering the passion of angels
Great wings spreading over Triton
Knowing before knowledge became dust
Inexorable power beyond the soul
Subsumed in magic waves
Stretched to the clouds
Casting nets of grace
To slap the seven seas
Gathered together
In one howl

Waiting in Emptiness

The streets stretch out
Empty like rivers without boats
Sky stretches above
Full of clouds
Empty of sunshine
The inexhaustible ocean rests
Bathes in cleaner waters
Nearly empty of industrial refuse
People like turtles
Draw back their heads into their shells
Become nearly invisible
As they wait
As they watch sky and ocean
Become bluer
And air clearer
As they imagine
Walking into a more pristine world
And vow to preserve
That cleaner world
While they wait in emptiness now
And wonder

April Moon

Beautiful moon of April
I have looked for you
Full moon of April
Easter moon
Last night I saw your halo
Blushing through the pink night sky
Pushing light into a dark city
Last night I lay under your light
Hiding behind veils of darkness
I felt the souls of the dead
Breathing

Riffs

Riffs suggest songs of childhood
Songs of yesterday
Brief clusters of notes remind us of London Bridge
September in the Rain, Getting aboard the A Train
To take a little trip around a city now mourning her dead
Not from wars nor collapsing buildings
But from a tiny enemy
Tiny and lethal whom we must avoid
Like the plague she is
Highly contagious
Sending her missiles throughout the world
Global pandemic via ships and après ski
Shelter in place stay home wear masks
Wash hands and wash again and again and again
Ashes ashes, all fall down
Humpty Dumpty rhymes with another name
Sat on the wall, had a great fall
All the kings' horses and all the kings' men
Nothing could put him together again
A tisket a tasket, on the way he dropped it
He dropped it
Dropped six weeks of testing
Carriers with no symptoms
Continued to infect
Four and twenty black birds baked in a pie
Smoked in lies and injustice
Court decisions force Wisconsinites
To choose between possible death
And standing in line to vote
Absentee ballots voided
Print tons of money
To keep the nation afloat
Shelter in place
Float on a boat of King Tide debt
Row row row your boat
Life is but a dream

A Bog in Spring

Sea grass clumps moistly
Soft cushions for ducks
Climbing out of muddy waters
Wet shores speak of sunshine
Whispering softly of spring
Ringing bubbles rise
Through damp floating leaves
Greeting willows
Dusting frog sprawled rocks
Enjoying damp warmth
Lure swarming insects
Through pollywogs
And boggy depths
Caught in a sparkling instant
By a turtle's timely tongue

Shoreline Stroll

We walk along the shore
Toes curling sand
Matching footprints
Just ahead
Tiny puddles
Small signs of peace
March towards the surf
Disappearing in dampness
Wings escape a lapping tide
Riding upwards
Feathered wings
Meet soft etched clouds

Ossianic Vapors

Ossianic vapors question tension
Earth peers up from sea mist
Wondering at life above her crusty face
Clouds dance across blue
Drops of rain splash across hot lava
Forests emerge in silence
Green sprouts become giants
Tender green blades cradle flowers
Surprising earth herself with brilliant hues
Beauty and perfumes
Wrinkling her forehead she creates mountains
Across her brow march animals
Her hands full of lakes and seas
Living creatures find the water
Crawling out upon her land
Finding ways to dwell upon her bounty
Gambling through the tawny hairs of earth
Following her streams
Dipping once again into her palms
Emerging onto mud and sand
Discovering fire and stones
Some walking upright learn to dance
Finding hands to beat and carve
Mouths to blow on pipes of reeds
Laughing back at mother earth
Slumbering under and within her masterpiece
Feeling life begetting life pulsing deep within her veins
Flowing onward ever onward as she spins and twirls
Rolling through space with wings of lace
Spun by her angels hiding in the clouds
Covering her labors with ossianic vapors
Embroidered into dreams

Touch of Clouds

Nimbus mist augers rain
Damp darkness swells
Wet laundry hangs over the horizon
Dripping from
St Francis' imaginary clothes lines
Birds chatter and hide
Mourning lost sunshine
We chatter to ourselves
Or to others on Zoom
And then hide
Mourning lost human touch
A bear sits in my window
Waiting for children to wave
From the street
A stuffed bear
Among other bears
In a collective neighborhood
Entertaining children
With stuffed bears
Placed in windows
For them to find
Walking from bear to bear
Discovering connection
In a world of silos
Isolated individuals and families
Sheltering in place
So as not to contaminate one another
And yet taking children into the street
To find bears
Sitting silently
In one another's
Windows

Mayflower and Disease

Disease has always challenged humankind
Even the Mayflower
Departing England 6 September 1620
Arrived Cape Cod 9 November
With half its crew and passengers
Scurvy, pneumonia, tuberculosis
Maybe a coronavirus tucked into the misery and death
Diseases picked up en route
Plymouth
Holland
Hudson River
Already native peoples resisted the English arrivals
Forced to return to the Mayflower
Anchored at last in new Plymouth
To mourn their dead
To begin a new life
Of immigrants
Immigrants to a new country
Unwelcome aliens
Whose history
Was still to be written
In the blood of error
And courage
Loss
And redemption
Disease
And healing
The never-ending cycle
Of civilization
Destroying and building
Unwelcome
On strangers' land

New Deal for a New World

Hoover took a radio job near the end of his presidency
Needing the money as his nation teetered on disaster
Millions without jobs and financially desperate
Thousands of banks closing
States prohibiting cash withdrawals
Hoover sure this was due to public fears of a new president
Franklin Delano Roosevelt, inaugurated March, 1933
Fell on his way to the podium, scattering the pages of a short
Poignant address with ideas heralding a New Deal
Re-nominated in 1936, he compared royalists who colonized
To new royalists who tyrannized our material wealth
Making no room for small businesses and workers
Roosevelt declared our nation must be freed of tyranny
To climb out of this deep depression
We must open the nation to social ideas
Worker relief, bank reform, agriculture support, social security
So that we might thrive
With a new infrastructure built to support the people
Today a similar threat of economic collapse
Merges through the ravages of a tiny virus
Morphing into a pandemic
We question our president
Once host of a TV show
Who seeks excuses for inept responses
Like Hoover coveted financial reward
And like none other covets adulation
As in his show The Apprentice
Enjoys firing his advisors
Yet has no answers
Even in tweets
The nation must choose a president to guide us
Into a post-pandemic world
Built on another new infrastructure with new answers
That abjure the tyranny of corporations and wealth
That support the safety, well-being and freedom of the people
That is built on truth and justice for a new world

Potomec for Earth Day

I am Patawomeck
You know me as Potomac, river of swans
Ten thousand years I was home to native peoples
Living near what is now your Capital
I have seen settlers come and kill our people
Paddle our waters and bring diseases and pollution
But I know sun and beaver, swan and dolphin
Sharks have plied my waters, bringing me stories of the ocean
You call me Atlantic
I hear stories of generations
Even the Greeks who tell me Atalanta
Was the fastest runner in Athens
A girl worthy to share an ocean's name
My many arms embrace the land
Embrace the people
Pollutants run down my cheeks like tears
Years ago someone cared, dared to name Earth Day
To clean my waters
Fifty years and I am not yet clean
A plague ravages my shores
People cannot visit and play on my banks and waters
Until a virus leaves
My history has been written in disease
Since the white man came
Disease killed my tribes
My currents are swift yet feed my fertile banks
Emptying into Chesapeake Bay, named by the Algonquin
Bay of oysters
Once killed by pollution
Oysters return again to Chesapeake
To celebrate with dolphin and with deer
With petals and with plants
Now I wait for the virus to disappear
And Potomac to remain clean
When people visit me again
To enjoy my waters

Wing of Trust

Her wing casts a shadow
Brief
Flying with her thoughts
Glancing against walls
Murmuring through clouds
Dancing over contrails
Painted against blue
Whirring as she brakes
Wings reversing
Her tiny torso leans back
To land
Believing earth will welcome her
Trusting air and light and land
Knowing no betrayal
Existing in faith and joy
The shadow of her wing
Disappears
With the sunshine of her world
Disappears with the promise
And constancy
Of sunset

Food

Hurricanes, floods, locusts, Covid-19
Who will plant, who will harvest what is left
What is left of the crops of earth?
Perhaps three hundred million people
Walk slowly towards starvation
Many millions already walking or floating
Away from Iraq or Yemen, South Sudan, Myanmar
Guatemala, El Salvador
Fleeing wars and violence
Nursing new babies on the islands of Greece
Looking to the other side of the world
The world beset by locusts and hurricanes
Look to Kenya Somalia Ethiopia
For sustenance, for food
Who will harvest the world's crops?
Mexico devastated by Covid
Further frustrated by blocked borders
Blocked from work
Fruit remains unpicked, wheat ungathered
Supplies sit in warehouses
Failing trucks to pick up and deliver
Grocery shelves empty
Restaurants closed, non- essential workers told to stay home
Climate extremes devastate homes and farms
Cyclones blow fierce winds as polar ice caps stretch and crack
While continents shudder from famine and disease
Refugees continue to flow out of countries
Where they are not welcome
To other countries
Where they are not welcome
Who will plant crops in yet fertile fields?
Who will cultivate those fields?
Who will harvest, gather, distribute
There is no Little Red Hen to save us
She has no papers
She is not wanted
Who will feed my world?

Bay Sunrise

Today I saw the sunrise
Blinding me with its glare
Reminding me of its power
I turned again to explore the beach
Reaching for shells
Seeking Wandering Tattlers
Friends of high tides
And clear ocean murmurs
Swimmers dotting the bay
Laughing as gulls squawked
And Wandering Tattlers
With their long beaks
Hid in rock crevices
Waited to drink from
Clean fresh waters
From dawn's tidal rush

Love

Love is multiple
Love is present
I love my child
I love children
Existentially
Philosophically
Emotionally
Love is infinite
Therefore love is equal
If I must clothe my child
I must clothe all children
Or do my part
That all children be clothed
I love those whom I love
Those whom I love
Are infinite
Therefore I must love all

Old Wisdom

We speak in many languages
As nature talks in the speech of the wind
And raging oceans
The light of sun
The scent of roses
The crush of snow
And crystals of ice
Our speech floats in the air
Conveying only what is received
Layered in dissonance or harmony
Over words or thoughts
Jangled untidily among us
The moon asks us to observe
Floating space
Her craters and valleys
Say little
Cradled in silence drifting above
River cascades below
Tumble and carve
Valleys and mountains
Throwing rocks
The mallet of Michelangelo
Discovers artistry
Hidden in deep quarries of Carrara
Great spirits embrace old wisdom
While we layer animus over animus
Forgetting to be still and listen to our hearts
Beating quietly among tangled debris
Pounding gently through conflicts
Sinking into earth with homo naledi
Precursor of compassionate Neanderthal
Arms outstretched with ancient compassion
Yet layered again with war or simple quarrels
Spoken in many languages
Yearning to break free, to sculpt a new world
Forged and molded with old wisdom

Spaces Between Ideas

Spaces between ideas
Stretch
As we hover between lines
Translating language
Into abstracts
Intimation more cogent
Than exactitude
Feelings impossible to transmit
Lit with perceptions
Questions intended
Inconsequential
Nonessential
We hang between lines
Of spirit and intent
Denting the line we inhabit
Like a hammock
Swaying between thought and substance
Distance betraying conflict
Between heart and mind
Wanting to believe a space
Of our own imagining
Reading between lines
We inhabit in our hammock
Tense with ropes
Holding us
Hanging
Suspended

Black Coffee

Music lives in spaces
We live in paces
Cups of black coffee
Walking the floor
Watching the door
Living in sounds
Tones
Rests of anticipation
Alienation
Spaced paces
Waiting
Coffee cools
Music spools into
Unknown chords
Unexpected relief
Or resignation
Beyond memory
The light is soft
A single lamp in the darkness
Glows through the window
At empty streets on a Saturday night
Chill summer air
Fills a void of dark
Cloudless night skies
Anonymous creatures hurry by
Laughter muffled by masks
Soft scuttle of children's feet
Sound of an ambulance
Stillness

Giants on the Earth

Giant viruses
Roam the earth
A smaller molecular world
With its own dinosaurs
In their world they were too small
To see another world evolving
From stone and water and iron
Afraid of oxygen
Found only in pockets of earth
Often flooded out with tides
Yet harnessed by some ambitious molecule
While viruses kept silent
Riding any hosts they could find
Playing with hydrogen and water
Tiny viruses as well kept pace
Sometimes replicating on pieces of themselves
Puzzles chewed off into puzzles
Waiting as the other world evolved
Waiting for their chance to ride new species
Algae and fungus rode each other
Melting into lichen
Inhabiting great woods in synergy
Viruses hijacked species
Abductors and destroyers
Adapting to destroy yet still preserve their host
Parallel worlds evolve to create and devour
Microcosms of good and evil
Demon and angel
Finding balance everywhere
Life spreads
Throughout infinity

Agony of Demeter

The mountains are too high
The shadows long
Daffodils are far too bright
Nightly angels whirr like hummingbirds
To tell me she is gone
Lured away into a story
Told upon a meadow
Where she played
I watched her dance among the flowers
Until she disappeared
Leaving a whisper of intensely sweet
Pomegranate hiding in the grass
Angel hummingbirds, lead me to her
I walk into the darkness
Nine years into darkness
Seeking my Persephone
Mortals turn me out when I would make a little boy a god
I mourn and all the meadow turns to dust
The meadow where she played
Autumn buries all the fruit she ate
Till winter cools the world
Death walks with me nine years as months
Yet in her stillness she returns
To kiss my cheek
And give the meadows flowers
Until the dust returns
And I retreat
And wait again
For springtime

The Rose

The rose unfolds
Miraculously
Soft petals
Infinitely fragile
Stretch
Open
Pour fragrances
Perfume of life
Purpose unexplained
Known to bees
Hummingbirds
Nectar seeking
As natural
As our breath
Pulses
Rhythmically
Softly beating
Unaware
Of being

Fire

Fire talks
Warmly
Welcoming
At a campsite
Or fireplace
Cleans debris
Surfeit of forest
Makes room
For new growth
Fire crackles
Burns
Devastates or heals
As does
All of creation

Country Walk

Walking in the countryside
Leaves crackling underneath
Smell of fresh breath of growing things
Soft fingers of the wind
Curling through my sleeves
Pat my face
Open my eyes
To grace
Trace my steps
With cool
Laughter

Squirrel

A squirrel races up a tree
Paws knowing each crevasse
Of bark and limb
Seeking storage spots
Hiding acorns
Chattering to the breeze
Squeezing into holes
Cradling new life

Whimbrels

Whimbrels fancy whimsy racing quickly towards retreating tides
Sliding beaks into the sea drenched sand recovering bits of
Landlocked protein hiding within shells
Children find sand dollars out upon the beach
Reaching everywhere like stars on star washed shore
Whimbrels run and peck race tides and dive their bending
Crescent beaks
Into wet sand avoiding or ignoring dogs and bipeds strolling on
the land
As screeching gulls soar effortlessly above the whimbrels
dancing racing
Pecking prancing poking crescents to retrieve their feast
I stroll in my own world of whimbrels
Fancying I were a bird
Unheard of joys awaiting me in flights so close to shore
Among my kin expecting a great soar into a sky
Devoid of clouds yet full of whimbrels
Sated with our meal
Stealing upwards towards the north
Feathers, flight and I

Forever Aloneness

Imagine aloneness forever
We know of a turtle, a frog, a rhinocerous
Maybe twenty or more animals
Who are the last of their species
Alone
Without hope of a species companion
Alone
More than isolated
Perhaps knowing
They are the end of the line
Perhaps not
Yet fumbling along
As they grow old
In the high risk group
Vulnerable
Not immune
To disappearance
To extinction

Everywhere Virus

It is everywhere
A virus is there
Tiny molecules float in the trees
Rest in the breeze
Curl onto my knees
Suck with the bees
Nectar and lees
Of pressed wine
Dining with me
Sliding off soap
Into glistening drains
Feeding through lanes
Of trash and leaves
Everywhere
Filling the air
The virus is there

Evening Gold

The golden evening washes into empty streets
Touching the city with a magical paintbrush
Pigments of light shine on silken bristles
We watch the shadows sliding through twilight
Hear the fog horn bellow while fog pushes its way
Across a mourning city
Covering constellations
And hiding the moon

Indifferent Nature

Looking at the clouds
I see the boot of Italy
Move across the sky
Thinking of a new old continent
Discovered under Eastern Europe
I wonder how many nations
Live on top of a lower crust
I wonder about earth's history
As I look up at the clouds
Floating over a world of viruses
Indifferent to their ancestry
The clouds already have morphed
Into new dwelling places of air
Now stringing whispers and rags
Over soft blue
I wonder how our virus guests
Have morphed into more or less
Virulent forms of themselves
I wonder how many in Africa and China
Look at the clouds
And see reflections of the world
Pass by in a blue sky
While they wait for an indifferent virus
To fly away or settle for another season
Somewhere under clouds resembling
Soft floating beds of angels

I Walk Under Redwoods

I walk under redwoods
Seeing their long journey towards the sky
Their bark remembering centuries
The birds remembering where to perch
I smell the scent of pine and mint
And see a warbler hiding under flower flurries
Seeking insects or nectar
I stand under redwoods and sky
Asking if they grieve or rejoice
With those who walk beneath
I gaze up at their green embroidered hands
Swaying gently in the forest breeze
I hear them whisper songs
Of sorrow and of joy
I walk under redwoods
Admiring their solid trunks
Remembering ages of storms and sunshine
I gaze through lacy soft pine needles
Reach for cones dropped through branches
To soft ground

El Polin Spring

I walk across a spring
Discovered by natives in a forest
Centuries ago
Home to butterflies and birds
Home to lupine and lilacs
Home to a quiet breeze
And hidden shelters
Under native trees
I walk across a spring
And look up at hills and forest
Circled by large birds
Serenaded by warblers and jays
See hummingbirds whirr
And dash upwards like tiny rockets
I walk across a spring
Admiring stone benches
And foundations of a village
Sheltering peoples of a past time
Whose shadows still evoke
Ghosts of a spirit world
Meditating
At a rippling spring
Where warblers and woodpeckers
Still bear testimony
To their ancient memories

Layers of Dandelions

We live in a world of layers
Crumpled history crushed under new ideas
Fertilized with rust and humus
Inquiline lace stitched and embroidered
By dandelions brushed under throats of children
To evoke memories of yellow butter
Thin parchment spider webs glistening with dew and sunshine
Hide burrows of voles, hide doors to nests of birds
Nature's playground on layers of history
Pushed under by paws of bears
Hooves of mustangs racing through ages
Unaware of yokes and ploughs
Layers of growth visited by hungry dredges
Heavy hammers and pressured water
Acids and poisons to extract ancient oils
To fuel machines leaving deep marks on layers of earth
Sending particles of burnt fuel, contaminating field of daisies
Layers reaching into our ozone stratosphere
Reaching back to eons of time under layers of native foundations
Bones of reptiles and vestiges of ancient fruits
Upwards to pumpkin patches
Bent steel of crumpled computers
Mystical small rectangles glistening among cords and cables
Where snakes slither, gazing upwards at tiny microbes
Layered miniscule vipers threatening human endeavors
Checks and balances push a pause button on new layers
Corona spins over fields of industry, resting on plastic and paper
Flying with human breath to infect and contaminate
As we have polluted the air of our only home
Now our own lungs are recipients of contamination
Reminding us of our mortality
Asking us what we will grow now
To assuage the peering snakes of virulence
To assure a new world
New layers of dandelions
Children's laughter and yellow butter
From flowers crushed under their chins

The Paintings

I walk inside each painting
I touch the flowers and people of Pissarro
People climbing on ladders to pick fruit
Children playing in the meadows
I lie down in their grass
Or the grass of Monet
Or look over the shoulders
Of Cezanne's card players
I walk among Rembrandt's crowd
Seeing Jesus for the first time
Insulted and spat upon
And want to embrace the people
And tell them the sunshine above is love
I walk upon Georgia O'Keeffe's petals
Jump among her clouds
Whisper to Cassatt's little girl in a blue chair
Join Renoir's boating party luncheon
Dance in Henri Matisse's circle of dancers
Or watch with Toulouse Lautrec's audience
At the Moulin Rouge
Walk Vermeer's little street in Delft
Stopping at the lace maker's window
To admire her work
Longing to rest
But simply gently push the hammock
As Gustave's Courbet's sleeper
Dreams
And slide away out of each frame
Of human joy and human pain
Into the other side of the mirror

Eel, Gift Wrapped

The most mysterious of animals
Born millennia ago in a unique sea without shores
The Sargasso Sea defined only by currents and inlets
Until the fingers of Gaia placed Panama across her waters
The palm of Gaia collected her seaweed
Within that seaweed growing eels
Born as larvae to drift thousands of miles
Floating and disappearing within gulf streams
Becoming transparent eels
Returning to Sargasso on those same streams
The Sargasso gyre, tangling sargassum weed
To nourish its marine creatures now gathering plastics
Caught in the vortex of that same gyre
An enormous garbage patch dangerous to turtles, eels and fish
Yet always welcoming its prodigal eels
Now mature to propagate again
Larvae to float thousands of miles
To become two species on either side of Panama
Nature's own call to diversify
Her snakelike creatures of the sea
Expanding northward and westward
In the mighty Atlantic
Venture to the Pacific to transform again
As giant Moray and the small eels of Hawaii
Together with their brothers from the Sargasso
Trust the ocean and her goddesses
To protect and nourish
While bathing them in micro-plastics
Floating like enduring rot
Suffocating life without its knowledge
Slowly strangling the ocean
While her angels of the sea
Traveling thousands of miles
Find their ancient home
Usurped and dying
Gift wrapped in plastic

The Gap

I am a giant cavern across which you must leap
From one world to the next
Across which you must swim or fly to find your way to peace
The world you leave is angry
Tangled with greed and steel
Breathing hatred and pollutants
The world you leave is beautiful
Yet suffocating with all you heap upon it
It cries out to you
Leave me to resurrect
Leave me to walk in beauty again
Leave me while you seek another world
That you may treat with tenderness
You are not wanted as you are
You have not matured
Yet are not children
You must become innocent again
Fly away
You are not wanted
Until you learn to live with beauty
Cast away your greed
Throw away your golden calves
Melt your idols
I am a giant cavern
You must find your way to the outer banks
Of a new world
Only then when you have lost your greed and fake idols
Lies and yearning for power and wealth
When you have disrobed
And cleansed yourselves of selfish effusions
Greed's illusions
Transformed your poisoned effluence into sweet honey
Nectar welcomed by bees and hummingbirds
Ceased from desecrating the land, air and water of your world
Only then may you return
And I will close the gap and welcome you

I am Durga

I am Durga
I am the breath of
Brahma, Vishnu, Shiva
My body made by gods
Deity of arms twice five
I thrive on ending pain
In eternal battle with
The dark side of the mirror
The desert of creation
Where demons dwell
To persecute good
I am the weapon
Destroyer and creator
I am Mahamaya
Mother of all
I am Durga
I merge with the universe
I surge with the sea
Leaving the world of evil
On the lion of good
My three eyes reflect my trident
Peace is my desire
Action is my power
My third eye is fire
It burns with knowledge and destiny
My arms embrace the world
Welcoming to peace all who have nothing
For they will be filled
Welcoming to justice those who are wronged
For they will find peace
Welcoming to mercy those in pain
For they will dwell in the lotus
As all gods and great souls of the spirit world
Dwell in the lotus
Fruit of purity, fruit of Ganga
Fruit of light

Yearning to Breathe Free

She stands there
Torch held high
A gift of the French
At the close of the Civil War
In honor of our Emancipation Proclamation
In honor of the freeing of slaves
Her hand was to hold broken chains but grips a tablet inscribed
with the Date of the Declaration of Independence
Her famous words written by Lazarus
To earn money for the pedestal
Were written and inscribed in 1883
Yet how fitting to remember huddled masses
Yearning to breathe free as we mourn and rise in anger
Over the death of George Floyd and Eric Garner
And all who have been choked, asphyxiated, murdered
By an unjust, oppressive society
And a president who would turn his armed forces
On the people he represents
Who protest the laying of a knee
On the throat of George Floyd
Family man, basketball coach for kids
Rapper, human being
Called a "gentle giant"
How much better the laying on of hands
Of all those oppressed by our nation
To confer a new blessing
A new hope on our tattered and crying country
Yearning to break free from its chains of war
Its legacy of slavery
Its hatred of the other
Who is in reality
Ourselves
Undeserving
Yet desperately in need of
Our own blessing
Abjuring death by police knee
For life by hands of justice

Ice

I am a polynya
I am an oasis in a desert of ice
I am a little pond
I am a trough of food for animals
I disappear and reappear
I have seen a billion years of ice
I live in the Arctic and the Antarctic
I have watched ice disappear around my edges
As I watch ages come and go
A billion years and more
I nourished the beginnings of new animals
Walking on two legs
Walking over bridges of ice
To live around me
To live beyond me
Great winds blow away ice
That might consume me
So I remain a refuge
Yet bipedal animals with tools
Have become clever
And dug into the earth
Bringing up old reservoirs
To burn for heat and energy
Making my home hotter
My ice walls melt
Glaciers about me calve
My world becomes smaller
Bipeds bring ships to study me
Yet keep burning
Keep heating my air
My sides melt more quickly
I wait for another winter
Where ice and wind make me whole
I cry cold tears
And curl into my warming breath
Melting into a suffocating planet
Whose life I nourish
Whose breath disappears
Each year a little more

Sequestered methane and carbon
Give me time to breathe
Yet as my friends around me melt
Those gases leak into our world
They wrap us up
In suffocating
Blankets
As they have done before
Till I
And all the world
Can't breathe
Can't breathe
Can't

Catch

Catch a falling sun
Right there
At the horizon
Burning
Radiating energy
Yet softly acquiescent
To the tumbling algorithms
Of our universe
Catch a falling universe
Whirling like a gypsy
With a skirt of nebulae
Swirling infinitely
Catch an infinite idea
Lost in the song
Of a sparrow

The Great Turtle

The Iroquois called it Anowara:kowa
The Great Turtle
Because of its shape
Others called it Vineland or Winland
Or West Indies
Amerigo Vespucci
The first to realize
This was not West Indies
But a new land
Amerigo Vespucci
Lent his name to it
America
It came to encompass all of the north
And the south
North America with Canada
And South America as far as Chile
America
Perhaps we need a new name
For the United States
Land of disappointment
Land of hope
Land of change
I for one
Would love to live on the back
Of a Great Turtle
And subscribe to the legend
Of the Great Turtle
Lying on the back
Of turtle upon turtle
Reaching up to the sky
Reaching upwards
Ever upwards
Breathing the clouds of truth
The clouds of knowledge
Clouds of compassion
Surrounding
The Great Turtle
Anowara:kowa

My Pocket

I put a piece of sky inside my pocket
Very small
I don't think anyone saw me take it
Except perhaps a chickadee
Who rested on a branch
Upon a tree
In front of me
And shook his head

I put a piece of forest in my pocket
Light as air
I don't think anyone saw me take it
Except a chipmunk
Who ran so fast
Up the tree trunk
Trying to hide himself
From my theft

I put a piece of dirt inside my pocket
I don't think anyone saw me take it
Grimy humus
Smelled like heaven
Mushrooms, rocks and earthy things
Maybe worms
Things to save and to remember
Years of childhood

I put a piece of ocean in my pocket
I don't think anyone saw me take it
Made believe it wasn't wet
But full of dreams
Of rocks and waves
And what now seems
To me to be
A symphony of life
Of you and me

I put a piece of you
Inside my pocket

I don't think anyone saw me take it
Except perhaps you saw me
Look up to the sky
And out to sea
So maybe you
Know I love you
And keep you
Always
In my pocket

Hold the Moon

Try to hold the moon
Like a discus thrower
Send it through the night
In your dreams
Try to ride the moon
Through a starless sky
Catching moonbeams
On the way
Ride it past the sun
Dip your hand into
The pool of sunstreams
Ringing round your moon
Brunnhilde singing in the ring
Of Wotan's torch
Lean into the moon
And out into the fire
Blending myth and magic
Sending dreams around the moon
And into fiery lace
Racing inwardly towards light
Embracing fire
Embracing space

Yoga on the Wrong Side of the Mat

Friendship built on forgiveness
Misunderstandings creating chasms
Intimacy foregone through misplaced yearnings
Time finding itself on the wrong side of healing
Dealing its own mixed cards
Confusing aces and jokers
Queens and jacks
Losing in their conquest
Against a loaded deck
Extra cards
Wandering orphans
Lost in foreign hands
Fifty-two pick up
On an uneven playing field
Walking through life's scattered deck
Doing yoga on the wrong side of the mat
Which card is this?
Just guess
All is illusion

Song of the Finch

I hear the song of the finch
Trills and variations
Songs rivaling the beauty of its vocalist
Orange headed breath of life
Flying more quickly than its song
A spark emulating the flash
Of a shooting star

Star Time

Clouds ride by like dreams
Dreams in the mirror of night
Sliding over a milky way
Resplendent in robes of time
Swirling folding countless years
Of light and speed and space
Our moment but a sparkle
Yet infinite in brilliant grace
Dropping stardust on our hearts
Drops of pain and joy
A mark of time deleted
Life so brief
A beat
A moment lost
While questions seem erased
In one embrace

Unwinding

Thread unwinds clockwise
Minutes flow by
Like rivers
Always downstream
Try to rewind the thread
Counterclockwise
Like swimming upstream
Each painful stroke
Lost energy
Crawling over stones
Reaching for hold and purchase
Wanting to go back
While every moment touched
Moves on
Moves past
Life continues to unwind
Our words
Endeavors
Errors
Cannot be retrieved
Yet neither can the beauty
Of the rushing stream
The threaded tapestry
Remembered joy
Replete inside our bones
Neither can that
Fail to forgive

Smoke and Dominos

Smoke in the sky
Wildfires
Birdsong at dawn
In a sultry sky
Particulate pollution
Pervades
While global unrest
Invades a world
Of outrage
Voices scream of murder
Built on lynching
Abuse and slaughter
Through the ages
Echoes and re-echoes
Property the domino
That must be saved
While human lives
Black human lives
Fall to their graves
Pieces scattered
With indifferent ease
Killed with knees
Hands casually in pockets
Dominos just that
Worthless pieces
Dipped in blood
Ripped from streets
In silent innocence
Made to suffer
Dominos of flesh
Wrested from hate and apathy
Played with for stakes
Unworthy of any game
Of any law
Of any social system

Solar Strike

Sun refuses to get up
Tired of her blue world
Wanting to say
You're on your own
I won't be part of this
Yet a balanced universe
Demands her presence
Reluctant she appears
Behind a veil of gloomy skies
Wanting to strike
Stop the world
I want to get off
She cries in vain
As forces greater than her own
Wind up her fiery splendor
Make her march across the sky
Across her earth
Created blue and pure
Enduring human wrong
A striking sun would rectify
But must go on
As universal gears and pulleys
Yank a disenfranchised sun
To serve an undeserving world
She would refuse

Hemispheres

Hemispheres compete over eons of time
We see one side
View constellations on our side
Ignore the other
As stars and black holes
Nebulae and star fountains
Pour away and through our skies
Imagine suspension floating above the earth
As she turns and we enter on invisible carpets
Into opposite air
Imagine voyages of ships exploring oceans
Hemisphere into hemisphere
North Star Polaris disappearing with its dipper friends
While a new sky enters star by star
Planets visiting on moving orbs
Southern Cross demanding space
To be our guide
We on our invisible carpets
Navigate another place
Remembering each universe
Of known and now discovered brilliance
Separate and strange
Wiser are those birds or eels
Who travel through each hemisphere
Yearly following a wandering sun
Knowing a home on either side
As we now navigate on sky ships
Strangers on our journeys
Neighborhood to neighborhood
Yet for our travels are not wise
Fail to accept
The universe is one

Refashion the World

We protest in the streets
Black lives matter
Immigrants matter
Homeless matter
In the prisons
Brown and black and white do battle
Who shall matter
Who shall shatter histories
Of misplaced hope
Scattered dreams
To piece together
Dream by dream
All colors of the rainbow
All life nourished on earth
That all may thrive
We protest violated lives
Unredressed grievances
Unmitigated loss
Unanswered sorrows
We pound the earth with anger
Yet she cannot help
The dreams we must refashion
Thread by thread
Rag by rag
Until we all together
Fashion a new world

Little Things

Do we remember little things
The flutter of a sparrow
The soaring of her wings
The birthing of a butterfly
Emerged from her cocoon
Wondering at her wonder
To see a world so vast
Yet knowing somehow
She must seek her destiny at last
The scent of drops of dew and petals
Carpeting her path
To daisies, lilies, lupine, roses
Daffodils and dandelions
As she and bees and hummingbirds
Each visit those sweet beauties
Do we remember touch
Do we remember light
Escaping through a canopy of trees
On summer days
Or shooting stars
Twilight before the night
Golden hours of mystery
Before the sun would set
In soft pastels or brilliant hues
Embrace of wind at dawn
Your face your smile
Your clear blue eyes
Too precious to forget

A Morning Dream

I curl into a morning dream
As birds accompany my thoughts
I see them soar
I curl into a morning dream
Seeming caught between the songs of birds
And time
I curl into the orbs of space
Stretching bending hours
Beyond passing knowing feeling
Bouncing on a tongue of fire
Understanding burning as a concept
Wrought in runes
I curl into a book of letters
Burned into a morning dream
Seeming caught between the stars
And time
Squeezed into a trine beyond all angles
Moving illusions of a clock
Ticking far beyond
All nebulae
All orbits
Pushing
Bending me into
A trine that layers
Extra edges of a universal pie
Irregularly cut
Yet pieces that
A giant relishes
Crumbs of never
Spilled into a giant's maw
To redirect a ticking clock
And curl back into time

I Lie Within a New Moon

I lie within a new moon
Rocking gently in the night
Drinking from the Milky Way
Scattering its light

I lie within a new moon
Rolling in a sea
Of stars and clouds and nebulae
Floating over me

I lie within a new moon
Blanketed with skies
Glowing beams of sunset
Fading from my eyes

I lie within a new moon
Gazing at the sky
Wondering what the night will bring
Me, the moon and I

Hadrosaurs of Old World

Striding through snow under giant forest pines
Hidden deep in the arctic
Bathed in northern lights
Bones upon bones upon bones lie remembering
Edmontosaurus family of hadrosaur
Prey to tyrannosaurus rex
Duck billed herbivores with a thousand teeth
Milled grain in their mouths as they walked
As they lived and dreamed in a cold world
Fought their way across deep sandy rivers
Cascades and swift currents
Too slow to escape the crocodile
Yet walked in heavy numbers
And now are found in fossil graves
Bones once buried rattling in graves of the Cretaceous
Singing songs of death
Songs of methane gases
Flooding their plains and forests
Creeping up from frozen beds
To stretch and embrace and suffocate
An earth of dinosaurs
Surprised to see a duck-billed platypus
Escape his giant family
The little hadrosaur creeping carefully away
Away into the sea
Away from lethal gasses
Finding Australia in a Paleolithic moment
Warm blood and tough eggs
Furry hair keeping him cozy
A tiny body like a cat with paddling paws
And a bit of poison on sharp heels
Giving him access to a new world
And strange creatures of his mammalian family
Who admired his bill yet could not believe his age
Of over 110 million years

Neanderthal

I dream dreams
I cannot write or speak
Except in small syllables
But my large brain
Is full of ideas
I know in my haze of thoughts
You gave me a name
To study and understand me
I am you and something else
I lived 400,000 years ago
Some of us were here even before
But met you 40,000 years ago
Before one day I disappeared
Or was subsumed in Homo sapiens
Subsumed in Druids
Subsumed in you
My ancestors crossed the globe
From Asia to Europe
Following the setting sun
Across land that is now lost
We lived in the land of the mammoth
Whom we hunted
While we learned to grow grain
We learned to make fire
We learned to cherish each other
To cherish our loved ones
To put flowers on their graves
We learned to dream
I dream of Druids
Following the sun
To make circles worshipping
Movements in the sky
To build huge slabs
To track time and the sun
To worship light and the solstice
You call it Stonehenge
Another they made of wood
Woodhenge, you call it
To track the seasons

Like those records you call calendars
I see in dreams
A large circular village
Buried near Stonehenge
Where someone lived and loved
Like us and like you
Someone who built stone temples
I dream dreams
Dreams of ideas
Dreams of thought
Dreams of knowledge
Dreams of language
And I will survive
Until I am lost in you
And I become
Your dream

People's Budget

Lloyd George and Churchill hand in hand
Fought for the people's budget
Passed by the House of Commons
Not by the House of Lords
Fearing taxes on them and their land
Fearing obliteration
Fearing equality among all people
Yet incrementally change happened
As populations clamored for health care
Once given them by monarchs
Now demanded of the state
England after Germany
Whose Bismarck system
Collectively protected all the people without profit
Regulated by law to be fair
Insure that everyone had dental care
Mental, physical care and baby clinics
Special weeks for bonding between parent and child
Curative weeks for vulnerable populations
All of Europe protected its people
And the world took notice
Beyond Castro's Cuba
Early on an icon for social equality and health care
Spreading its doctors to vulnerable countries
Till those people too were all protected
The old world moved from health
To social well being
While the wealthy of the new world
Looked on and feared obliteration
Feared equality among all people
Feared taxes and loss of land
Feared the equity demanded by our Constitution
Yet now the peoples' protests
Of murder by police to protect property over people
May finally corral an oligarchy
Powered by injustice

The Virus is Not Weary Yet

The virus is not weary yet
Happy to be sociable at protests
Or big events and rallies
Feeling stifled confronted by masks
And shunned by distanced walkers
Yet clinging to a hope of transfer
To some unsuspecting traveler
To a welcoming hand or face
The virus and his family have thrived
Through eons
Simply being patient
Today the wind runs naked through tall trees
Bending branches
Howling over chimneys and rooftops
Pausing for a breath
Then bearing down again
With howls of pleasure
Free to wrap itself around
Each eucalyptus trunk or cedar branch
To whisper sweet expressions
To its feathered friends
Who take a ride upon its gusts
Or seek shelter in a shallow eave
To wait for it to tire
Wind clothes itself in rags
Scatters abandoned clothing
Reaches for huddled sleepers
Maskless beggars sitting on a curb
With cardboard hoping for a dollar
Impervious to viruses dancing in their midst
Infections spike while people gather
Protest closure
Protest murder
While police crimes multiply in times of anger
Injustice asks both voice and solidarity
The virus joins the crowd
Happy to oblige

Unique Vision

Each sees a halo around the moon
Hexagonal Ice crystals
Bending sending rays
To each of us
Individually
I see a halo around the moon
As I see around you
Uniquely
Your sight of the halo
Is your own
As my sight of your beauty
Is my own
We see a rainbow
All its colors through a prism
Uniquely
My rainbow is my vision
Your rainbow yours
The rainbow I see after the rain
The halo I see around the moon
My own
My own vision
Of you
The rainbow
And the moon

The Timing is Off

The timing is off
Love was behind the curtain
But no one opened it
So it languished
Sitting on the windowsill
With the wind and the birds
Singing to itself
Seeing the sun go down
And feeling the night winds
Waiting for the dawn
Yet sensing itself dissipate
Before the sunrise
Like dew on spring leaves
The timing is off
Like snow arriving late
When April's heat
Melts its attempt to spread like powder
On hills of green and gold
So turns it into moisture
Resembling tears
And yet
The timing is off
And tears can find no place
While there upon the windowsill
The wind and birds
Sing untimely serenades
And music turns to glass
Upon the window

Quantum entanglement

An atomic cascade
Photons divide
Yet remain mirror images of each other
Traveling apart
Each counterbalances the other
One spins to the left
The other spins to the right
Perfect compatibility
Carbon dioxide into oxygen
Oxygen to carbon dioxide
Photons of photo-synthesis
The universe spins one way
While another universe balances
We imagine our half of a photon
Occupying a random space
While the other half
Occupies its alternate dimension
Entanglement means embrace
Do we embrace as opposites?
Do we embrace our mutuality?
As oxygen needs carbon to regenerate
All of nature intermingles
In mutual necessity
Cascades of atoms
Reach across universal divides
Even love transcends itself
In mutual embrace
Across eons of uncharted space

Dark Matter

Ghosts of the universe
Dark matter
Unseen yet present
Essential energy
Unobserved gravity
Pulling like invisible taffy
On all corners of space
Ancient pre-creation
Primordial
Black holes without limits
Like the Sargasso Sea
Written in chalk
Edges ever smudged
Blending into the universe
Dented with planets or meteors
Even with stars born or dying
Lying upon dark essence
Denting it as on a hammock
A blanket ready to slide like fog
Into unknown spaces
Silly putty claiming all timelessness
All energy beyond light
Invisible yet essential
Pushing against gravity
Forcing life to evolve
In unfathomable waves
Dark oceans of the universe
Enormous ghosts like hands of god
Holding us in space kneading energy
Pushing against time to create thought
Pods and anti-pods
Molecules for giant children
Cosmic ghosts playing with their blocks
Fashioning clay forms
Into breathing life

Compatibility

I hear the moon had had enough
She had discovered after all these years
She and the earth were simply not compatible
It was time to move on
Similarly, even the Milky Way, a nation unto itself
Was through being eye candy for earth
And voted to move on to another universe
The earth, getting into the spirit of the time
Told the sun to get out of her way
She was packing her bags
Ready to move to a new galaxy
She wanted some excitement
Maybe a binary star
Saturn's rings felt let down by Saturn
Who had never recognized their beauty
And were being wooed by another planet
They felt was far more compatible
And certainly more grateful for their presence
If only they could figure out how to escape
Years of psychological abandonment
Down on earth Rorschach blots were
Re-examining their relationship
Discovering they had never been compatible
And were determined to divorce
Eager to distance themselves
While the very clothes I put on this morning
Had decided to escape, knowing they were not compatible
And belonged on a different skin
The onion skin heard their complaints
And tried to peel itself off its onion
Creating a torrent of tears felt throughout the universe
As an ocean of sadness compelled a lonely violin to play
To play music of the spheres to an ocean of tears
To play to the universe until harmony
Was restored

Stardust

Riding on piece of a star
Stardust bound by quarks
Holding on tight
As a dragon in the universe
A black hole with invisible teeth
Bites and splits me in two
Keeping my twin
While I escape back into the universe
Joining my piece of star
Swirling through exploding light
Spinning in emptiness
Spinning through galaxies
Until I ride to a Baobab tree
On a mystical planet
My star rests on its huge trunk
Remembering back
Thousands of years
When my star was a rose
Beloved by a little prince
Who rode back on stardust
Rode back on a snakebite
Covered in the petals of the rose
Monkey bread fruit in his backpack
Circling the universe
Warming the universe
With the beating of his heart
While I become the Baobab tree
And the star

Moon, Cheese and Mice

The moon was high in the sky at dawn
Its waning side exposed, vulnerable
As if a giant celestial mouse had bit a chunk
From the cheese of the moon
Leaving ragged tooth marks
The moon sighed down to earth
Perhaps we need a cat in the sky
To scare the mice
Back into the Milky Way
Where the cat
Could curl his tail
Around his favorite beverage
And pounce
Just occasionally
Upon a celestial
Mouse

Checkers in the Sky

The stars were playing checkers last night
Black holes lining the board
Facing bright stars
The black holes seemed to be winning
Until a king jumped over a star
And fell in love
Looking at her starry eyes
Wanting to embrace her
Part of her fell into his arms
And part fell off the board
As just so happens
When stars and black holes fall in love
While playing checkers
Half the star sought her sister
And the black hole king
Wondered what had got into him
But his wife's twin sister
Sent her love in brilliant rays
Around the loving pair
In warm embrace
And all the checkers
Black holes and white stars
Danced upon the night
Soft shoe on velvet checkerboard

Go Gentle Into that Good Night
(Inside the mirror of Dylan Thomas)

Go gentle into that good night
Go with ardor, go with thought
But do go gentle into that night
Rancor and anger hate and stress
Will not allay the heart's distress
Winnow your soul and find its core
Seek to be grateful, to adore
The beauty and the pain of life
Walk through the barbed gates of strife
Go gentle into that good night

Lie down in pastures green and gold
Walk through the valleys now grown old
Through shadows calling you to rest
To think to muse to wish the best
For all you love for all you miss
Fearing no evil wishing a kiss
On all that walk with you this night
Walk gently with you into light
Go gentle into that good night

Go gently into that good night
Think mildly back on all you sought
To win to gain to hope yet look
On those who joined each step you took
And think on them you loved who loved
You too with awkward heart and view
Their gift so sweet and fresh imbued
With hope and faith and joy and light
Walk with them into that good night

Go gently into that good night
Tread on the stuff that falls from dreams
That laughs and whispers on your path
And on the pebbles in life's streams
Remembers when your heart was new
Catching your tears like morning dew
Breathing with every step you take
Grieving each loss, each pain, each ache
Lifting your spirit, thought and sight
Walk gently into that good night
Go gentle into that good night

How Long?

How long before
We destroy monuments to crime
How long before we erase the glory
Vested on the rogues of our history
The founders and leaders of the Ku Klux Klan
Those who held hundreds of slaves
While they spoke hypocritically
About the evils of slavery
How long before we end the lies
Lies glorifying heroes who oppressed the people
Founders of our nation
Who spoke of freedom
Yet sent armed police after their own escaped slaves
Who herded up native peoples
Sending them on the trail of tears
Who brought disease to those same peoples
Erasing most of their population
Who killed the buffalo and deforested our country
How long before
We reckon honestly with our history
And cease honoring those who dishonored
Every principle ensconced in our own documents
Our Declaration of Independence, our Constitution
By denying their fundamental message
Freedom and equality for all
First by diluting that principle
By defining black Americans as less than human
Until an amendment righted that wrong
Later killing them for registering to vote
After the Civil War gave them full rights
How long before we cease to glorify
Those who dragged their feet
On the abolition of slavery and segregation
On granting full rights to women and minorities
Cease to glorify those who built our railroad
On the backs of Chinese slaves
Sent in poorly woven hammocks
To lay thousands of rails
Often falling to their death

Do we have a monument to the Chinese
Who built our railroads?
Do we have monuments to the slaves
Who created our rich nation
Through their blood, sweat and tears?
Do we have monuments
To the heroes of the Underground Railroad
And those who risked their lives fighting segregation?
To those who called the murderers
Of our black citizens to account
Though they themselves might be murdered?
It is time we end the glorification
Of the ugliest chapters of the history of our nation
And begin to celebrate those who fought
That our nation become its own dream
It is time that we begin to make America great
It is time that America become
Not a beacon on a hill
But a humble emissary in a valley of hope
Asking directions of its true martyrs and heroes
That it may not again lose its way

Legacy of Africa

Camel caravans still plod the desert of humanities' first centers
of learning and civilization
Through the heart wrenching twilight hours they walk against
the sun
They walk across the Aksumite Empire
Breathing in the dust and gold, bearing the scrolls and art of
ancient libraries
Ethiopia, Eritrea, Dijibouti, Egypt, Saudi Arabia, Somalia South
Sudan, Sudan, Yemen
Names we know today once part of a great empire nurturing the
first blossoms of civilization
Names we know today birthed the fertile intelligence that spread
across the globe
Birthing the Aztec, the Maya, the Greek and Roman great human
minds and thoughts and art
Emerging from over 10,000 years of farming, emerging and
evolving language, dance, ideas
Their empire becoming one with China Persia Rome feeding the
world new thoughts
Their camels connecting the land to the sea
Their stelae still stand
The obelisk of Aksum and the chapel of the Ark of the Covenant
Still visited in Ethiopia
While from Mauritania, Senegal, Mali
Camels brought their wares and priceless thoughts to the
Mediterranean
Along with gold from the Kingdom of Ghana
Camels from the Wagadu kingdom connected all of the Sahel
While Koumbi managed a huge population with limited water
through engineering
Trading their cola nuts, origin of Coca Cola
Before the great Mali civilization subsumed Koumbi
Gambia, Guinea, Gunea-Bissau, Ivory Coast, Mali, Mauritania,
All the Mali empire
Mined half the gold of Africa
Its emperor Mansa Musa perhaps the wealthiest man the world
has ever known
Spreading trade routes throughout Africa
Spreading until inevitable conflict tore away at his empire

127

Songhai controlled the waterways of the Niger
Soon the new empire, building on reservoirs of intellect
Influenced by wandering tribes of Tuareg natives
Built the great library of Timbuktu
Becoming the academic center of Africa
Extending into Spain and Turkey via Morocco
The blossoming of Islam with the animist cultures of Africa
Encouraged acceptance of all cultures and religions
Under the embrace of Islam
Epitomized later in Ronda, Spain, center of religious diversity
Yet the Songhai empire was threatened by a eunuch from
Morocco
Whose sultan wanted a great empire
Nearly achieving it at the battle of Tondibi which crushed the
Songhai empire
By outnumbered Moroccans with the arquebus, the original
shoulder powdered weapon
Still the nomadic Tuareg remained with their stories and their
love of the desert
Their stone huts and exquisite ornaments and dress and their
noble white camels
The salt mines they controlled
They with other nations formed the Kingdom of Great
Zimbabwe
Only gradually crumbling to colonial invasions from the west
Encroaching on civil conflicts and unrest
Exploiting the evolution of African slavery and the disintegration
of kingdoms
To erode the great civilizations of Africa
Never to be forgotten
Never to be erased from human endeavor
Today, tomorrow and forever

Ethiopia

A musician is assassinated
In Abu Dhabi
Haacaaluu Hundeessa
Mourned by thousands
Who follow his coffin
Loved by the people
Born in Amba, Oromio
He helped give voice to
The Oromo people after
Over 150,000 had been expelled
From their homes by Ethiopia
From 10 million Oromo
Are now 5 million
Their numbers reduced by genocide
The Oromo saw hope in Haacaaluu's songs
Hope in the young man
Who led them
Who kindled their spirit
Until his own was murdered
Yet remains in the hearts
Of the Oromo
Who continue
To sing his songs
And see his vision
For their people

CAMEOS

Fog

Fog blankets London
Slides beneath tall buildings of Dubai
Creates mysterious veils around Stonehenge
Swallows up the Golden Gate
Dances with ghosts in Newfoundland
Spins around the Eiffel Tower in Paris
Rolls about canals of Venice
Bathing gondolas in singing mist
Throws feather beds about the buildings of New York
While fog horns bellow out its presence
To ships at sea
Lending sound to foggy mist

Shadows

My lamp sways
Throwing shadows everywhere
My own shadow I see against the wall
Becoming larger as I approach
Until the wall is only shadow
The closer I am
The less I see of my shadow's shape
The farther away
The more I see
The shadow attaches itself to my feet
And I stand
With my shadow
Outlined upon the wall
Before me

Monarchs

One day monarch butterflies
Landed on our garden in Lake County
Hundreds of monarch butterflies
I thought they'd stay
Not fly away
So I left them for awhile
Thinking I would join them later
Maybe take pictures
To remember a miracle
But when I returned the butterflies were gone
They had just wanted to say hello
To our garden
On their way south

Refrigerator Memories

The refrigerator is plastered with pieces of my life
Grandchildren, family, notes and artwork
I see it impossibly untidy impossibly complex
With love and thoughts of loved ones
A pastiche of poetry of family and friends
An echo of past joys and losses
Laughter and smudges
Magnets of birds and fish
Certificates, photographs and
Slips
Of paper
Left there so the refrigerator will not forget

Stuffed Bear

A bear looks out the window
A stuffed bear
He has been looking out the window
For many months
Since we began sheltering in place
For the pandemic
Nextdoor blog asked us
To put bears in the window
For children to hunt in the evening
When they take family walks
My bear tried to hold a sign
Saying Black Lives Matter
But it slipped out of his little paws
And now sits in another window

Balcony and Birds

Finches and chickadees and sparrows
Visit my tiny balcony
The finch eats seeds from a shell
The chickadee and sparrow hang
Or perch on my bird feeder
They sing or chatter
And seem to wait for friends or mates
Sometimes their friends are more important
Than the seeds
They want them to peck their fill
But when one flies away
The other follows

The Sound of Light

I wake up in light
Past sunrise
Light floods my room
Wind rustles through my open window
As if it were the sound of light
Smells of pine and cedar creep into the day
Becoming the perfume of light
As wind upon my cheek
Becomes its touch

Bruno

There is a bear
Wandering through Wisconsin
Iowa, Illinois and Missouri
Looking for love they say
Social media has named him Bruno
He has swum the Mississippi
Wandered through fields of soybeans
Made it across highways
27,000 people have joined the
Save Bruno club
And look out for him along his trek
As he looks for another black bear
To love

Rage and Art

Rage reigns against white legacy
Against white governments
Against white art and sculpture
Perhaps against white music
Bach Beethoven Brahms
Barber Britten Copland Ives
Gershwin Bernstein
Masters of jazz and classics
Along with their black counterparts
Not less remembered
In the great music of jazz and funk and classics
Billie Holiday, Ella Fitzgerald
Thelonious Monk, Jester Hairston, Prince
In prior ages the legacy of art
Was born by other races and lands
Often by slaves
Look in museums of art and history
It is all there and remains
The work of Africans often done by slaves
Chinese pagodas and silk screens as well
The great pyramids and sphinx of Egypt
Mastered by thousands of slaves
Directed by architects
Who themselves were sentenced to die in their own creations
Yet the creations remain
Testimony to the greatness of civilizations
If not to the justice of their systems of government
Art mirrors society
Right and wrong
Mozart, Puccini, Verdi, Bizet
Musicians and artists all call us to look at ourselves
Mimi and Rodolfo creating art while starving and dying
In the slums of Paris
Susanna and Figaro battling demands of the count
For the conjugal first night
With intelligence and grit and a revolution
Engineered by Mozart
Leonora as Fidelio
A woman disguised as a man

To free her unjustly imprisoned husband
A political prisoner
Injustice exposed by Beethoven
Messengers come with sculpture and music and poetry
To expose outrage, wrongs, and victories
Standing on street corners
In fountains and city squares
In museums and art galleries
Concert halls and opera houses
Throughout our nation and our world
For us to remember
The smile of the Mona Lisa and the Black Madonna
The horrors of Guernica
Evils of slavery and segregation
Porgy and Bess
West Side Story
The myths and fairy tales
The injustices, wars
Horror and glory
Throughout the ages
Art reminds us of our humanity
May we tear down idols of injustice
Memorials to leaders of the Ku Klux Klan
Memorials to those who upheld slavery and injustice
May we share the art of truth, memorials to truth
Continue to remember, continue to create
Art for the ages

Black Deaths by Covid

Slavery ended
Capitalism did not
White supremacy was firmly ensconced
And never buried
The black American might be more skilled,
Better self-educated, more talented
Nonetheless relegated by the system
To the lowest rung on the job ladder
Several pegs from a second rung
Three rungs above ripped out
Given the lowest rung on the housing ladder
Facing too many obstacles to rent or own property
Equitably with his or her white compatriots
Given the lowest rung on the health ladder
Far more apt to die as a mother or child in childbirth
On the education ladder
Facing discrimination in admissions and in the classroom
Today we see the results of that discrimination
Of being on the lowest rung of every societal ladder
We see the results in the high death rate from Covid-19
We see the results in the high death rate from cop killings
We see the results in the number of African Americans
Incarcerated in crowded prisons
Private prisons run for profit
Police hired to protect property not persons
And fill the prisons with chattel
It is time to put back the rungs on the ladders of life
So that everyone may climb
Everyone might extend a hand to those beneath
And help each other
Rung by rung into
A world of justice

Be Safe, Be Well

I read of locusts in Africa
In Somalia, and locusts in India,
Now a cloud of locusts in Argentina
Eating enough each day
To feed one half million people
Wiping out lifetimes of farming
As a virus we don't understand
Kills more people than ever before
And young people are named as main carriers
While they greet the world with smiles
And unmasked faces
Crowd the streets and laugh
Spreading droplets
That may overcome the hospitals
And a Sahara desert storm
Offering beautiful sunrises
And hazy skies
Drifts to Florida and the Carolinas
With clouds of dust
While we hunker down
Protect our families
And tell everyone
Be safe, be well

Nesting Herons

Enormous nest of Great Blue Herons
Blows in the bay winds
Regal mother stands look out
Guarding yet respectful
Of her brood
One adolescent heron
Ventures out
Lands in a small cedar below
Hobbling along its quills
To find balance among the branches
Finally escaping
To find respite in the sky
A path back to its nest
Sheltering in the Eucalyptus

Song of the Finch

I hear the song of the finch
Trills and variations
Calls rivaling the beauty of its vocalist
Orange headed breath of life
Flying more quickly than its song
A spark emulating the flash
Of a shooting star

Dream Petals

The wind cuts through my sleep
Roaring gently
As the sky drops rain
Comforting
Yet echoing
Her cousins
All around the world
Blowing chills
Inviting showers
As children huddle
Raindrops scuttle
To and fro
Wanting only to give life
Reassure the flowers
Wind and rain
Blowing pouring
Cutting through my sleep
Slumbering children deep
In dreams
Everywhere
Dare to fly on wings of air
Falling drops of hope
Greet a dawn
Wet with rain and newness
Caught in petals

Nonessential Time

The bird flies faster than the wind remembers
Encompassing a neighborhood in seconds
Or time played backwards
As leaves curl into nothing
And bears look out windows
For passing children
And butterflies live their short spell
With a flutter of beauty
While clouds merely are
And are not
And moon gets lost
Arriving in a sunlit sky
Unsure of where to go
Wishing to slip eastward behind stage
While the sun completes
Her performance
And disappears
House right

My Name Is Anyone

My name is anyone
They call me an unaccompanied minor
I had to leave my family in Guatemala
It could have been El Salvador, Honduras
Or even Mexico
I had to leave
Gangs threatened me and my sister
There was nothing to eat
I worry about my parents
I am cold here at the border
Except when the sun burns
And there is no water
No one seems to care
But there are many of us
I hear almost 80,000 came over last year
And more came with families
And were taken away from their parents
We don't know where our home is
There are many babies who have disappeared
Their mothers cry all the time
Some of us die
But we cannot go home
We are dreamers too
We want a home
Where we are safe
We don't want
To be forgotten

DACA

Finally
The Supreme Court
Rejects Trump's
Abnegation of immigrant rights
Children raised in the US
May remain
Dreamers may dream
Families may rejoice
Yet wonder
As they dream
As they rejoice
Why there was ever a question
Of their humanity
Of the reality
And value
Of their lives
And families

Olawatoyin Salau

Protested George Floyd's murder
By police
Named the names of those killed
By police
Named the name of a molester and rapist
Who had violated her
Was herself murdered
Salau was left on the street s of Tallahassee
Dead at 19
Where is the justice
If black men and women
Are not protected
Are not cherished
How many more names
Will we cry out
Over and over again
That they not be forgotten
When our own society
Witnesses their pain
Instigates their death
By those who should protect
But who allow
Or commit
Or fail to prevent
Their murders

Hidden Consequences of Covid

Under the blankets of Covid-19
Hide systemic injustices
Thousands of immigrant children
Detained far from their parents
Are lonely and afraid
Crowded into unsafe quarters
Without protection from an
Unseen ubiquitous virus
They have been forgotten
Victims of inconsequence
What is the redress
For a baby of four months
Taken from his mother at the border?
Or for his mother
Crowded into detention quarters
Susceptible to a virus
Worrying about her baby?
More is hidden under the blankets of Covid-19
Where work has stopped to address
The injustice of climate change
This year showing the highest CO_2 concentrations
In the atmosphere in three million years
Since before human beings walked our earth
416.18 per million mole fractions of air mass
Who knew?
The effects of polluted air devastate the poor
Afflict economically marginalized
Afflict black and Hispanic populations
Climate change is violence to the poor
To children suffering from ill health, asthma
Climate change is violence to the environment
To marine animals pushed north
To coral reefs eaten away by acid oceans
To our Arctic and Antarctic
And the pools they harbor to sustain life
To our ever calving glaciers
Under the blanket of Covid-19
Lie injustices and inequities
Police brutality exacerbated by

Social restrictions, curfews, unemployment
Due to a virus
Under the blanket of Covid-19
Lies much we are forgetting
As we isolate
From the real world
When the blanket is removed
What world will we see?

Birds on the Move

Dozens of birds sing and play
Among the boughs of my pear tree
As I yearn to join them in song and flight
The wind is slight today
Carrying their light bodies
Easily and tenderly
Among the blossoms and new green
As they balance on branches
Yielding and springing
Up, up they go
Into a cloudless sky
The crow sails south
Through clouds of gold
Washed by the sun
Her view of earth is vast
Seeing giant buildings
And flowering trees
Below
She still knows her way back
Back home
Wherever that might be

Yearning

Yearning speaks in the wind
Yearning turns in tender circles
Fledgling birds seek the air
Chatter among themselves
Surprised to find hummingbirds
Nearly their size fluttering
Whirring buzzing singing
Yearning in their tiny hearts
To exhilarate in the springtime
Sunshine yearns to warm the earth
Turns flowers towards her rays
As they yearn to open to light
To burn to turn to imitate
Their mother sun as sunflowers
Heavy with seeds yearn
To stretch to grow to spring above
The earth yearning itself to nourish
To burn to turn discerning yearning
For life's own burning churning pulse

Le Désir

Le désir parle dans le vent
Le désir se transforme en cercles tendres
Les oiseaux débutants cherchent l'air
Babillent entre eux
Surpris de trouver des colibris
Presque leur taille flottant
Chant vrombissant
Désireux dans leurs petits cœurs
Pour exalter au printemps
Le soleil aspire à réchauffer la terre
Tourne les fleurs vers ses rayons
Comme ils aspirent à s'ouvrir à la lumière
Brûler se tourner pour imiter
Leur mère soleil comme tournesols
Lourd avec des graines aspirent s'étirer
Pour grandir et s'élancer au-dessus la terre
Qui soi-même s'aspire à se nourrir
Pour brûler et pour discerner
Pour le propre pouls brûlant de la vie

Strawberry Moon

Strawberry moon
June moon
Full and bright
Your face disappears
In the darkness
The clouds walk by
Hiding you discretely
While you play with them
In the night
Now on earth
On the streets
At the seashore
Masked figures quarrel
In the darkness
Moon, beautiful moon
We beg you
Illuminate our world
Illuminate our souls and our thoughts
That all might live
In your light

Fraise Lune

Fraise lune
Juin lune
Pleine et lumineuse
Ton visage disparut
Dans la noire
Les nuages qui marchent par toi
Ta cachant discrètement
Pendant que tu jouer
Avec les nuages dans la nuit
À ce moment sur terre
Sur les rues
À côté de la mère
Figures masquées se quereller
Dans l'obscurité
Lune, belle lune
Nous prions à toi
Eclaire notre monde
Illumine nos âmes et nos pensées
Afin que tout puisse vivre
Dans ta lumière

Towers of Giraffes

Giraffes roam in towers
Like lions in prides
And geese in flocks
Towers of giraffes sleep at night
Necks over their backs like swans
One giraffe keeps watch over his tower
Their brown patterns turn black as they age
We think they are silent
But they hum to each other
A very low rumble like swarms of bees
They often eat from the tops of trees
Or drink by spreading their legs
To reach the ground
Giraffes are endangered
They have a rare skin disease
Linked to malnourished soils
That covers their legs and shoulders
They often chew on bones
To replenish their calcium
Not long ago when oil drilling
Threatened the giraffes in Uganda
People tied up a tower of giraffes very gently
And took them over the river to the other side
To be safe
Six thousand years ago
The emperor of China
Who loved to travel
And collect exotic animals
Docked in Bengal
Receiving a giraffe as a gift from Kenya
He took it back on his large boat
In China the court artist
Drew the beautiful animal
Who became remembered as a myth
Like a unicorn

Sweet Spring

The air is sweet
The smell of aging spring
Nascent no longer
But heady with the smell of ripe flowers
Jasmine, roses
A hint of basil
The air is full of bird song
Leaps in register and trills
Of the white crowned sparrow
Echo through the woods
A chickadee examines his shadow
Imitating each tiny move
Hops down to say hello to his shadow
Which disappears
As shadows do
While bird song trills
As long as spring is sweet

Mavi Marmara Tragedy

Twenty years ago
Mavi Marmara
On a humanitarian mission
In international waters
With other ships
Part of its fleet
With medicine and medical assistance
To help the victims of Israeli brutality in Gaza
Nearly at its destination
Mavi Marmara, a Turkish ship
Carrying dedicated persons from many different countries
With a single compassionate goal
Was attacked and nine killed
Later a tenth died of his wounds
Blood covered the deck of the Mavi Marmara
And tears from an old man wanting to go home
After years in exile from his beloved Palestine
Yet Gaza remains the densest prison in the world
Under hostile occupation by Israel
Who kill even those attempting to help
Traveling in international waters
Who have done little to aid their Palestinian prisoners
In time of Covid
Save for allowing them to convert factories to make masks
And protective gear
For buyers in Asia

A Dappled Sky

A dappled sky looks down bemused
Gathering its silken skirts touched with light
Still and unmoving
As the wind gathers beneath
On city streets and trees
Petals of cherry blossoms scatter
Reminders of rosy glory
Yet the petals remain
A carpet for empty streets
Quiet, serene, peaceful
Anticipating nothing
One blue glove sits in a gutter
While a broken white and blue mask
Sits bedraggled on the pavement
Waiting for nothing
Anticipating nothing
Under a dappled sky

Pursuit

The chickadee is a sweet little bird
Thought he'd found his true love with a call, with a word
But he did not pursue her, too proud and too shy
Now they both are alone in one tree, in one sky
Then our chickadee did find a sweet little finch
And he sought out his friendship you see, inch by inch
But his finch found a girl with a quite different hue
A little brown finch he would like to pursue
She yielded at last to his amorous quest
Now they talk to their young in a sweet little nest
While the chickadee and his would be bride
Remain quite alone in their tree in their sky
Except for those times when the finch leave their bower
To join with our chickadee for happy hour

154

Black Lives Still Matter

We haven't learned have we?
We thought the call Black Lives Matter
Would make a difference
Would stop the killing of black Americans
Through choke holds
Or throwing them with handcuffs
And leg irons and no seat belt
In the back of police vans
We remember some of the names
Amadou Diallo Manuel Loggins Jr.
Ronald Madison Kendra James
Sean Bell Eric Garner Michael Brown
Alton Sterling Freddie Gray
Yes, we remember a few
But we are still killing black men
For jogging while black
We are still killing black men
Through choke holds
By the knee on the neck
We have not learned
Black Lives Matter
With Coronavirus it is
African Americans
And the indigenous people
Who are the major victims
Along with the elderly
All of whom live in close quarters
And cannot distance
Those we have failed
And let die
By not responding
Those we have failed
And let die
By thinking they are dispensable
They Don't Matter
The burden of guilt lies heavy

Say His Name, George Floyd

Property has no personal being
Property is a thing
It does not breathe
Like George Floyd
Or Eric Garner
Crushed by police
After accusations of
Alleged and unproven
Small financial misdeeds
Miniscule next to the looting
Of minorities by corporations
And the truly wealthy
Banks bailed out
While poor suffer
And can be thrown under
And suffocated
Who does not understand
The words, "I can't breathe"
A call to resuscitate, to help
Where police
Guardians of the people
Instead turn against and murder
Those people it must protect
Who does not understand
Riots will ensue
Burning of property
Which has no soul
And does not breathe

Birdwatching while Black

Two Coopers
Christian and Amy
One a black bird watcher
The other a white woman
With a dog
Who runs unleashed
In Central Park
Christian asks her to leash her dog
She calls the cops
Saying a black man is harassing her
The cops arrive and take the dog
Amy was abusing
To a shelter
They apologize to Christian
He, a former editor of Marvel Magazine
Goes back to bird watching
Asking people on twitter
Not to bother Amy
She'd suffered enough
And was sorry

Storming of the Bastille

Only seven prisoners in the Bastille July 14, 1789
When revolutionaries seeking cannon and gun powder
Stormed the Bastille to free them
Resulting in their own deaths
As they found and shot cannons
As well as their own rifles
Killing Marquis de Launay, Governor of the Bastille
On a pretext to spark a revolution
Finding printing presses there
And calling them instruments of torture
Perpetuating myths of horror
Within a benign Bastille
Bearing memories of wealthy citizens
Held in luxury suites for punishment or safety
Built April, 1370 by Charles V
To protect Paris from the English
Its walls held four hundred years of memories
Until its storming in 1789
Yet now instead of fortifications
Against the British
Another engineering feat
The Eurostar built in 1994
Binds two great nations
Reaching London to Paris
In two hours and fifteen minutes
Just three kilometers from the Gare du Nord
To the Bastille
A chance to stop in the Eleventh Arrondissement
Along the Seine or at the Place de Republique
For lunch
Pour déjeuner et penser sur l'histoire du Bastille

A Blue Glove

A blue glove
Curls in the gutter
Handless
Alone
Not even a mask
Or another blue glove
To keep it company
Alone but not isolated
Soon to be squashed
By a truck
Or sprayed away
To find itself
Stuck on a gutter screen
Or sliding down a pipe
Into a river or ocean
Where it sadly
Becomes food for fish
Or flows out to a garbage patch
Somewhere in an ocean gyre
One lonely crumpled
Blue glove

Comet NEOWISE

A comet crosses earth's path
Never to be seen again for 8,600 years
She dazzles against a purple sunset
Her crust is new and brilliant
As she races through the sky
A plume following her
Colors chosen by the disappearing sun
Or an unseen prism reflecting violet
Wandering across our horizon
Then lost again in space

Inequity and Infrastructure

Twenty-six people
Hold half the wealth
Of the whole world
And people still are
Starving
Still are coming over on
Matchbox boats and plastic rafts
To escape starvation
Or violence or war
Another baby
Washed on shore in Kos
Like Alan Kurdi
Washed up drowned in Turkey
Five years ago
Every day families die
With babies and children
Crossing from Iraq or Syria
To Greece
I waited with mothers in Kos
With eight new babies
Waiting for a boat to Athens
They could no longer stay in tents in Kos
There was no sanitation no food no water
For their babies
Most of the world is scrambling for life
Most of the world needs health care
Most of the world needs
What less than one percent
Could give
To help create an infrastructure
On which the rest might build their lives

We Mourn

John and Elijah
Beacons of hope
Gracing our last generation
Speaking wisdom in congress
Holding a mirror before our eyes
To see what our nation has become
Is becoming and can become
John Lewis, member of Congress 33 years
Severely injured by police in Selma in 1965
Beaten and arrested in countless sit-ins
And demonstrations for justice
Told us when we faced a challenge
We could decide what was right or wrong
John left us yesterday
Yet left also his charge to us
If not us, then who?
If not now, then when?
Elijah Cummings
Dead eight months before, at age 68
Rose from poverty to become
The most eloquent speaker
Of the House Oversight and Reform Committee
Called by Nancy Pelosi our North Star
Guiding congress to rise to a higher purpose
Said in his last month, weak from ill health
When we're dancing with the angels
The question will be asked
What did we do to make sure we kept our democracy intact?
Did we stand on the sidelines and do nothing?
He asked when Freddy Gray was killed,
Did anyone recognize Freddie when he was alive?
Did you see him?
Before black men are made martyrs,
Do we see them or are they invisible?
Elijah and John made us see everyone
And seek justice

Menhaden

Menhaden
Could be called a throw away fish
Not great eating
A forage fish
Famous for eating phytoplankton
Keeping algae from contaminating
Our oceans
Menhaden
Live and spawn in the Atlantic
From Florida to Nova Scotia
Often leaving their eggs in Rhode Island
Menhaden are disappearing
Due to lower oxygen levels in the water
And disease
As with Covid
Close quarters bring contagion
Menhaden swim close
Have not been taught to distance
Nor wear masks
Menhaden are food
For large fish, whales and dolphin
They swim in large schools
And need protection
For our ecological balance
When they are lost
The ocean loses
Menhaden are humble
But essential workers

www.ingramcontent.com/pod-product-compliance
Lightning Source LLC
Chambersburg PA
CBHW071523170626
46811CB00007B/2934